GLUTEN-FREE VEGAN

BAKING

GLUTEN-FREE VEGAN

BAKING

Over 80 delicious gluten-free and vegan recipes!

With foreword by The Vegan Society CEO

Jasmijn de Boo

This edition published by Parragon Books Ltd in 2014 and distributed by
Parragon Inc.
440 Park Avenue South, 13th Floor
New York, NY 10016
www.parragon.com/lovefood

ISBN: 978-1-4723-4905-7
Printed in China

New recipes and introduction by Jane Hughes
Foreword by Jasmijn de Boo
New photography by Noel Murphy
Home economy by Penny Stephens
Cover and internal design by Geoff Borin

Notes for the reader

This book uses standard kitchen measuring spoons and cups. All spoon and cup measurements are level unless
otherwise indicated. Unless otherwise stated, individual vegetables are medium and pepper is freshly ground black
pepper. Unless otherwise stated, all root vegetables should be peeled prior to using. Garnishes, decorations, and serving
suggestions are all optional and not necessarily included in the recipe ingredients or method. The times given are only
an approximate guide. Preparation times differ according to the techniques used by different people and the cooking
times may also vary from those given. Optional ingredients, variations, or serving suggestions have not been included in
the time calculations.

Where the author has made all reasonable efforts to ensure that the information contained in this book is accurate and
up to date at the time of publication, anyone reading this book should note the following important points:-
Medical and pharmaceutical knowledge is constantly changing and the author and the publisher cannot and do not
guarantee the accuracy or appropriateness of the contents of this book; In any event, this book is not intended to be,
and should not be relied upon, as a substitute for advice from your healthcare practitioner before making any major
dietary changes; Food Allergy Disclaimer: The author and the publisher are not responsible for any adverse reactions
to the recipes contained herein. The statements in this book have not been evaluated by the U.S. Food and Drug
Administration. This book is not intended to treat, cure or prevent any disease. For the reasons set out above, and to
the fullest extent permitted by law, the author and the publisher: (i) cannot and do not accept any legal duty of care
or responsibility in relation to the accuracy of appropriateness of the contents of this book, even where expressed as
"advice" or using other words to this effect; and (ii) disclaim any liability, loss, damage or risk that may be claimed or
incurred as a consequence – directly or indirectly – of the use and/or application of any of the contents of this book.
The publisher has been careful to select recipes that do not contain animal products or ingredients with gluten. Any
prepared ingredients that could potentially contain animal products or gluten have been listed with "vegan" and
"gluten-free" so readers know to look for the vegan or gluten-free versions. However, always read labels carefully and, if
necessary, check with the manufacturer.

Contents

FOREWORD FROM THE VEGAN SOCIETY'S CEO,

JASMIJN DE BOO

I believe it was on the first birthday after I became vegan, just over ten years ago, that I tried to make a cheesecake with silken tofu using a recipe that I found somewhere online. Unfortunately, some of my guests were not very impressed. I had either not stuck to the precise measurements or I might have substituted an ingredient for something that was not available. The result was edible, but not very appealing.

However, it doesn't need to be this way. In the last ten years, we have seen more and more vegan baking recipes being shared, loved, and praised, including by thousands of non- or not-yet vegans. Vegan and gluten-free diets are increasingly popular; however, whatever your diet, we all share a common interest in wanting to cook, eat, and share tasty and varied treats.

Whether you are cooking for yourself or for a friend or loved one, *Gluten-Free Vegan Baking* will be a great addition to your cookbook shelf. The instructions couldn't be clearer, so no more tofu cheesecake disasters for me. For those with a sweet tooth, there are plenty of ideas here, such as Chocolate Mint Marble Cake or Caramel Peach Bars. Fruit lovers are served well with recipes such as Apricot & Apple Spiced Loaf, Fig Upside-Down Cake, Orange & Cinnamon Muffins, and White Chocolate & Raspberry Tarts. And I am sure that the interesting inclusion of breads and other not-so-sweet baked goods, such as Cheese & Chive Bread, Beet Muffins, and Herb Biscuits, will make this unique collection popular.

I wholeheartedly recommend this book to you. The variety and flavors are the most inspiring I have seen in any vegan and gluten-free baking book to date.

Jasmijn de Boo

CEO, The Vegan Society
www.vegansociety.com

WHY EAT A VEGAN AND GLUTEN-FREE DIET?

Interest in both veganism and gluten-free food has rocketed over the past few years, for a variety of reasons, and an increasing number of people are looking for recipes that check both boxes. Vegan food is acceptable to a very wide range of people and ensuring that the food you offer is also gluten-free means that almost everybody can enjoy it!

THE VEGAN DIET

Veganism is often seen as a logical next step for vegetarians, as many vegetarians feel uncomfortable about the industrial-scale farming increasingly involved with the production of milk and eggs. The vegan diet does not include any foods of animal origin and most vegans extend this principle to other aspects of their lifestyle, by avoiding clothing made from leather or wool, as well as toiletries, cosmetics and cleaning products that contain ingredients derived from animals or that have been tested on animals. As awareness of the vegan lifestyle increases, it is becoming easier to find products of all kinds that are suitable for this ethical choice.

Although most vegans opt for this lifestyle for ethical reasons, believing that a plant-based diet is better for the environment, better for their health and kinder to animals, there are some vegetarians who tend towards a vegan diet not through choice but because of food intolerances or allergies related to dairy products or eggs.

THE GLUTEN-FREE DIET

Most people who follow a strict gluten-free diet do so for medical reasons. For those with serious conditions, such as celiac disease, eating gluten can cause a reaction that is both painful and dangerous. For this reason, it is essential that any food that is sold as gluten free is truly safe for those with serious allergies or intolerances. But there are a growing number of people who are experiencing milder intolerances to wheat and other foods that contain gluten. Many have found that they have trouble digesting these foods and have adjusted their diets accordingly.

Food intolerances vary widely, with some people finding that they can tolerate small amounts of gluten, or that spelt, an ancient variety of wheat, seems easier to digest. Over many centuries, the wheat that we grow has been modified by selective breeding to give it desirable characteristics, such as hardiness in the field, resistance to disease and a predictable pattern of growth and ripening. Some argue that modern wheat is now so far removed from the plants that used to flourish in the wild that it can barely be said to be a natural food and many people believe that this is the root of their dietary problems.

It is also true to say that the typical Western diet contains far more gluten than it used to – how many of us sit down to toast or cereal for breakfast, cookies at coffee time, sandwiches for lunch, and perhaps a slice of cake or a granola bar in the afternoon before our main evening meal? If that main meal is a pie, a tart or a pasty, a stew with dumplings, a pancake or a flatbread, something cooked in or topped with breadcrumbs, or pasta or a pizza, then we may well have consumed gluten at every meal. We may not even realize that the food we are eating is made with wheat, as wheat products are widely used in all kinds of TV dinners and may not be obvious, unless you check the list of ingredients on the package. Over-consumption of any kind of food can tend to precipitate unwanted reactions as the body struggles to cope with an overload, and, in the long term, a sustained overload can lead to a sudden serious reaction or a permanent allergy.

VEGAN AND GLUTEN-FREE BAKING

Baking without gluten presents some challenges. Gluten-free pastry can be crumbly and, without gluten, breads and cakes may not rise well. Many gluten-free recipes tend to rely on eggs to overcome these problems but, of course, that is not an option for vegan bakers. This book contains tried-and-tested recipes developed using a variety of techniques and ingredients to make sure your vegan, gluten-free cakes and bakes are successful.

VEGAN AND GLUTEN-FREE BAKING TIPS

The first thing to do when you are aiming to bake vegan and gluten free is to make absolutely sure that you are using the right ingredients. There are stumbling blocks for unwary cooks who might assume that all margarines and all dark chocolates are suitable for vegans or that cooking without wheat is just the same as cooking without gluten.

It's also really important to check the equipment you are using. Experienced bakers may be in the habit of making substitutions, knowing that things will probably work out. But recipes without gluten and animal products can be less forgiving. So, here are some helpful tips:

- Use the right size of cake pan. Using a smaller pan could mean a thicker cake that will struggle to rise and a larger pan could mean your cake heats through too quickly and becomes rubbery.
- Follow the instructions about mixing ingredients. There may be good reasons why the ingredients are combined in specific ways (see also the note on baking powder below). Some recipes really benefit from being beaten in an electric food processor, whereas others give the best result when they are just quickly stirred together.
- Follow the instructions about lining pans—batters that contain egg replacer and xanthan gum can be particularly difficult to remove from unlined pans and can also stick to lining paper as they cool.
- Follow the instructions about cooling your baked goods. Some things need to cool before they can be moved, otherwise they will break. Other things need to come out of the pans quickly, otherwise they will "sweat" and become unpleasantly damp.

A NOTE ABOUT BAKING POWDER

Some standard commercial baking powders are not gluten free—make sure you buy a brand that is labeled gluten free. Baking powder is a dry mixture of a weak acidic powder (typically cream of tartar) and a weak alkaline powder (typically sodium bicarbonate). When liquid is added, the chemical reaction creates bubbles of carbon dioxide that will make your cake rise. In cake batters that contain eggs, the cake cooks around the

bubbles to produce a sponge. In vegan, gluten-free cakes, the bubbles can rush to the surface of the cake and burst without providing the rising effect.

If your cake is not rising, it may be because you have left the batter for too long before putting it in the oven. As soon as the wet and dry mixtures are combined and the baking powder starts to act, the cake should go into the oven. If there is any delay (while you spoon the batter into a pan or divide it among cupcake liners), lift up the baking pan and rap it on your kitchen counter once or twice immediately before you put it into the oven—you will see some bubbles burst on the surface of the batter. This simple tip will stop your cakes from rising too quickly and then collapsing before the cake is baked.

A NOTE ABOUT OVEN TEMPERATURE

The correct oven temperature is critical and it's very useful to have an oven thermometer that will tell you what's really going on in there. Most ovens maintain a "ballpark" temperature by switching the heat on and off, and in some cases this can result in a noticable fluctuation in temperature. When you preheat your oven, it may indicate that it is ready to use long before the desired temperature is actually achieved. As a rule, vegan, gluten-free bakes should be placed on a shelf in the center of the oven, not too high or too low. It's best not to rely on rotating cake pans between high and low shelves as you bake, because the rush of cool air that hits your cakes as you open the oven door can have catastrophic effects.

If you are baking a cake with several layers and you can't get all your pans onto the middle shelf at the same time, the best option is to make the cake batter in several batches. Cake batter that is left to stand while you wait for oven space will quickly lose its ability to rise. This can make baking layer cakes somewhat time-consuming, but if you want each layer to rise properly and all the layers to be equal, it's better to be safe than sorry. The same applies if you want to make a lot of muffins or cupcakes—don't multiply the ingredients up and then leave half the batter to sit in a bowl while you bake the first batch of cakes, instead make two or three separate batches of cake batter.

HOW TO BAKE VEGAN

Many vegans enjoy cooking and like to make their food from scratch, partly so that they know exactly what they are eating and partly because they prefer to eat plant-base foods that are fresh and not treated with any flavor enhancers or preservatives.

Many recipes are easy to "veganize," but baking is a science and attempting to customize recipes can lead to some unexpected results.

REPLACEMENTS FOR BUTTER

Many people prefer to use margarine instead of butter in cooking and making this switch seems straightforward. It is important to realize, however, that not all margarines are suitable for vegans—many still contain dairy products and some are fortified with vitamins that are derived from nonvegan sources. Some low-fat spreads contain gelatin and nonvegan lecithin, which are both added to improve their texture.

There are all kinds of vegan margarines and butter substitutes available, and new products are being developed all the time. Products vary, but margarines may contain more water than fat, and this can have adverse effects when it is used for baking. Some people who are vegan for health reasons are also concerned that margarine is not a "natural" product and often contains unhealthy trans fats. For these reasons, many vegan recipes use light vegetables oils, such as canola oil or coconut oil.

REPLACEMENTS FOR MILK

Soy milk was the first vegan milk replacement to be widely commercially available, but the market is expanding rapidly, with milks made from almonds, rice, oats, coconuts, and hazelnuts all becoming popular. Vegan milks of all kinds tend to contain less fat and more water than dairy milk, and this can affect results when baking. Soy milk has a particular tendency to curdle when vinegar or lemon juice is added and, although this looks somewhat unpleasant, the result is a useful substitute for buttermilk in vegan baking.

All kinds of vegan creams and yogurts are now being developed, many based on soy milk or coconut milk. These can work well when served with vegan cakes and other desserts, but results can be unpredictable when they are used in baking, with some products splitting and becoming watery. Coconut cream—available online—is satisfyingly creamy but high in saturated fats, making it more suitable for occasional treats than everyday use.

REPLACEMENTS FOR EGGS

Eggs have interesting properties when it comes to baking: they can help cakes rise, hold dough together, add a glaze, make a sponge springy, or a cracker crisp. There are a number of ways to replace eggs in vegan baking, and the best choice depends upon the result you are looking for. Some vegan muffin recipes use applesauce to add body and moisture to a recipe. Others may use ground flaxseed, which has a gelatinous consistency when mixed with water and can help create a spongy texture. Both of these ingredients are most successful in muffins, which tend to have a denser and chewier texture than sponge cakes. Commercial egg replacement powders can often help to make cookies crisp, give a lift to sponges, and can even be used to make vegan meringue-style toppings for pies. For glazing, soy milk or a mixture of soy flour and water can produce good results.

OTHER VEGAN SUBSTITUTIONS

Vegan bakers need to be careful with some other ingredients, too. Dark chocolate is not necessarily vegan and, although there are good varieties of vegan chocolate available (including substitutes for milk and white chocolate), these may behave unpredictably when heated, separating into an oil mixture or hardening into lumps. It's important to note that some brands of confectioners' sugar are made with dried egg, some cake sprinkles contain gelatin, and some food colorings are not suitable for vegans, notably cochineal (E120), which is derived from insects. Beet powder is a natural food coloring that produces a vibrant pink or red color, which is perfect for making icings or frostings but turns brown when baked in cakes that contain baking powder. Try decorating cakes with shavings of vegan chocolate, crystallized fruit, or sugar mixed with vegan-friendly food colorings.

Fruit can sometimes be given a wax coating that is made from animal products, so be careful to select unwaxed fruit. Sugar can also be produced using animal bones, so check the packaging to be sure it is vegan.

HOW TO BAKE GLUTEN FREE

Finding gluten-free food is gradually becoming easier and substitutions are generally straightforward. However, baking without gluten can be tricky, especially if you are not using eggs. Many gluten-free baking recipes rely on the use of eggs to help bind mixtures and provide the elasticity that makes dough easier to work and baked goods more likely to rise.

Anybody with a serious intolerance or allergy to gluten will be well aware of which foods are off limits, but for other people, it might not be so obvious. Wheat, spelt, rye, and barley all contain gluten, and oats contain a glutenlike protein that many people with celiac disease prefer to avoid. Wheat-base farina and couscous also contain gluten. Some baking powder is not gluten free and you will need to make sure you check the label. It's also important to realize that wheat free doesn't necessarily mean gluten free.

GLUTEN-FREE FLOURS AND STARCHES

- **Amaranth:** Best used as part of a gluten-free flour mix, it can improve the texture of gluten-free baked goods and also adds to the nutritional value. It has a pleasant peppery flavor.
- **Arrowroot:** A ground plant root that is used like cornstarch as a thickener.
- **Brown and white rice flour:** Brown rice flour is heavier and more nutritious than white. It is best used in combination with other gluten-free flours.
- **Buckwheat:** Despite it's name, this is not wheat and does not contain gluten. It has a strong, bitter flavor that works well in breads and pancakes.
- **Chickpea flour:** Also known as besan flour, it is made from ground chickpeas, and it is often used in Indian and Italian breads and baking.
- **Coconut flour:** Finely milled dried coconut, which is tasty but can be dense and dry. It is best used as part of a mixture of gluten-free flours.
- **Cornmeal:** Used in cakes and breads to help retain moisture, it also adds color, texture, and flavor.
- **Millet flour:** A powdery yellow flour with a sweet flavor that works well in muffins and sweet breads.
- **Potato flour:** A heavy flour with a strong flavor best used sparingly. Potato starch is a different product, which does not have a strong flavor and can add moisture and a soft texture to baked goods.

- **Quinoa flour:** Rich in protein with a pleasant nutty taste, it works well in cakes, cookies, and breads.
- **Sorghum flour:** It has a sweet, nutty flavor and works best with other gluten-free flours.
- **Soy flour:** Used mainly as a thickener, it adds a nutty flavor and a light texture to a mixture of gluten-free flours.
- **Tapioca flour:** A starch extracted from the cassava root, native to South America. It has a sweet taste and adds texture to a mixture of gluten-free flours.
- **Teff flour:** Made from a nutritious grain native to Africa, it has a flavor that has been likened to hazelnuts.

Finely ground nuts, such as almonds, hazelnuts, chestnuts, pecans, and walnuts, and seeds, such as flaxseed, hemp, and chia, can also be used in conjunction with gluten-free flours to change the flavor or texture of a baked good.

Each gluten-free flour has its own properties, with some being tasty but heavy, others light but bland, and for this reason the most successful gluten-free baked goods tend to be made with mixtures of different flours. It is straightforward to find these gluten-free flour blends in some larger supermarkets, in health food stores, and online, and the blends have been developed to create flours that give good results across a variety of recipes. However, if you do a lot of gluten-free baking, you might enjoy experimenting with your own blends and you might find that this saves you money, too.

Once you have your gluten-free flour blend, don't assume that you can use it in any standard baking recipe. Pastry made with gluten-free flour can be too crumbly to use, yeast breads do not rise well, and cakes made with baking powder may rise too quickly and then deflate before they are baked through. Stick to recipes that have been devised specifically for gluten-free flour. If you are going to bake vegan, gluten-free cakes regularly, a package of xanthan gum is a pantry essential. Just a tiny amount makes all the difference, helping pastries and doughs to hold together and stopping sheet cakes and sponges from being crumbly. But don't assume that using more than the recipe specifies will be a good thing—too much and your sponge cakes will be oddly rubbery.

CHAPTER 1

Cakes

Raspberry NEAPOLITAN CAKE

With three different layers and two kinds of filling, this cake takes time, but what better way to show somebody that you love them?

PINK LAYER

1 raw beet

¾ cup raspberries

vegan and gluten-free egg replacer, equivalent to 2 eggs

½ cup gluten-free soy milk

1 tablespoon vegan and gluten-free cider vinegar

1 cup gluten-free all-purpose flour

½ teaspoon xanthan gum

2 teaspoons gluten-free baking powder

½ teaspoon gluten-free cream of tartar

½ cup firmly packed vegan and gluten-free margarine, plus extra for greasing

1 cup vegan granulated sugar

1 teaspoon vanilla extract

VANILLA LAYER

1⅔ cups gluten-free all-purpose flour

½ teaspoon xanthan gum

½ cup vegan granulated sugar

2½ teaspoons gluten-free baking powder

1 cup gluten-free soy milk

⅓ cup canola oil

2 teaspoons vanilla extract

CHOCOLATE LAYER

1⅓ cups gluten-free all-purpose flour

(ingredients continued on page 19)

1 Preheat the oven to 350°F. Grease three 9-inch cake pans and line with parchment paper.

2 For the pink layer, trim, peel, and grate the beet and put it into the bowl of a food processor with the raspberries. Process until smooth. Make up the egg replacer in a small bowl according to the package directions and beat it with a fork for a minute, until bubbly.

3 Put the soy milk into a small bowl, stir in the vinegar, and set aside to curdle. Put the flour, xanthan gum, baking powder, and cream of tartar into a large mixing bowl and stir together with a wooden spoon. In a separate bowl, cream the margarine and sugar together and beat in the egg replacer and vanilla extract.

4 Stir the soy milk mixture and the creamed margarine mixture into the dry ingredients and mix thoroughly. Pour in the beet puree and stir together with a wooden spoon until the batter is thoroughly combined.

5 Spoon the batter into one of the prepared pans and smooth the top. Bake in the preheated oven for 25–30 minutes, or until a toothpick inserted into the cake comes out clean. Turn out onto a wire rack and let cool completely.

6 For the vanilla layer, put the flour, xanthan gum, sugar, and baking powder into a large mixing bowl and stir together with a wooden spoon. Add the soy milk, oil, and vanilla and stir together until just combined. Spoon into one of the prepared pans and bake for 20 minutes, or until golden and springy to the touch. Turn out onto a wire rack to cool.

7 For the chocolate layer, repeat step 6, including the cocoa powder with the dry ingredients.

⅓ cup vegan and gluten-free unsweetened cocoa powder

½ teaspoon xanthan gum

½ cup vegan granulated sugar

2¼ teaspoons gluten-free baking powder

1 cup gluten-free soy milk

⅓ cup canola oil

1 teaspoon vanilla extract

VANILLA-RASPBERRY FILLING

2 tablespoons packed vegan and gluten-free margarine

¼ cup firmly packed vegetable shortening

3 cups vegan and gluten-free confectioners' sugar, plus extra for dusting

1 teaspoon vanilla extract

2–3 tablespoons gluten-free soy milk

2 tablespoons freeze-dried raspberry pieces, plus extra to decorate

1 cup fresh raspberries

CHOCOLATE FILLING

2 tablespoons packed vegan and gluten-free margarine

¼ cup firmly packed vegetable shortening

2⅔ cups vegan and gluten-free confectioners' sugar

⅔ cup vegan and gluten-free unsweetened cocoa powder

2–3 tablespoons gluten-free soy milk

8 To make the raspberry filling, beat the margarine and vegetable shortening together with the confectioners' sugar and vanilla. It's easiest to use an electric mixer, but you can do it in a large mixing bowl with a fork. Add a little soy milk, if necessary. When the mixture is smooth, stir in the freeze-dried raspberry pieces.

9 To make the chocolate filling, follow step 8 but add the cocoa powder at the same time as the confectioners' sugar. When all three layers of the cake are cool, assemble the layers. Spread the pink cake with the raspberry filling. Add a layer of fresh raspberries. Sandwich with the chocolate cake and spread over the chocolate filling. Finish with the vanilla cake and decorate by dusting with confectioners' sugar and sprinkling with freeze-dried raspberry pieces.

Cook's tip

Each layer of cake should be mixed and baked separately so that the baking powder is still active when it goes into the oven. If your cake shows any signs of sagging in the middle, pile in some extra raspberries to hold it up.

PREP TIME: 25 minutes COOK TIME: 45–50 minutes SERVES: 8–10

Chocolate & Banana LOAF

Chunky almonds and semisweet chocolate pieces give this cake its home-baked character.

- vegan and gluten-free margarine, for greasing
- 2 cups gluten-free all-purpose flour
- 2 teaspoons gluten-free baking powder
- 1 teaspoon gluten-free baking soda
- ⅔ cup firmly packed vegan light brown sugar
- 3 ounces vegan and gluten-free semisweet chocolate, coarsely chopped
- ¾ cup blanched almonds, coarsely chopped
- 3 ripe unwaxed bananas, mashed
- 1 cup almond milk
- ½ cup canola oil
- 1 teaspoon almond extract

1 Preheat the oven to 350°F. Grease a 9 x 5 x 3-inch loaf pan and line the bottom with parchment paper.

2 Sift the flour, baking powder, and baking soda into a large mixing bowl. Stir in the sugar.

3 Stir the chocolate and almonds into the dry ingredients.

4 Stir the bananas into the dry ingredients, along with the almond milk, oil, and almond extract, and mix well with a wooden spoon.

5 Spoon the batter into the prepared baking pan and smooth the top with a rubber spatula. Bake in the preheated oven for 45–50 minutes, or until a toothpick inserted into the center of the cake comes out clean. Let the cake cool in the pan for 15 minutes, until firm enough to handle, then transfer to a wire rack to cool.

Cook's tip

Many gluten-free cakes of this size will benefit from the ingredient xanthan gum to prevent a powdery texture, but the mashed banana does the work in this recipe.

Maple & Pistachio
BUNDT CAKE

This simple cake is wonderful with vegan and gluten-free vanilla ice cream and a fresh fruit salad.

1 Preheat the oven to 350°F. Grease a 9½-inch bundt pan.

2 Put the flour, sugar, and baking powder into a large mixing bowl and stir together. Finely chop one-third of the pistachios and set aside for decoration. Coarsely chop the remaining pistachios and stir them into the dry ingredients.

3 Put the soy milk into a small bowl and add the oil, maple syrup, and vanilla extract.

4 Pour the wet ingredients into the bowl of dry ingredients and quickly mix with a wooden spoon until just combined. Spoon the batter into the prepared pan and smooth the surface with a spatula. Bake in the preheated oven for 30–35 minutes, or until firm and golden. Let the cake cool in the pan for 10 minutes, then turn it out onto a wire rack to cool.

5 To decorate, transfer the cake to a serving plate, drizzle with maple syrup, and sprinkle the reserved pistachios over the top.

2⅓ cups gluten-free all-purpose flour

1 cup vegan granulated sugar

3¾ teaspoons gluten-free baking powder

⅔ cup shelled pistachios

1¼ cups gluten-free soy milk

½ cup canola oil, plus extra for greasing

3 tablespoons maple syrup, plus extra for drizzling

1 tablespoon vanilla extract

Cook's tip

Use the best-quality maple syrup you can—the taste makes all the difference when it's drizzled over this simple cake.

Cook's tip

Try substituting vegan rum for the amaretto to make a rum and raisin cake.

Almond & Amaretto CAKE

*This moist and tasty almond cake is great served with a scoop of
vegan and gluten free ice cream and a drizzle of maple syrup.*

1 Preheat the oven to 350°F. Grease an 8-inch square cake pan and line with parchment paper.

2 Put the golden raisins into a small bowl with the amaretto and let soak for 30 minutes. Make up the egg replacer in a small bowl according to the package directions and beat it with a fork for a minute, until bubbly.

3 Put the vegan margarine and sugar into a large mixing bowl and beat together with a wooden spoon until creamy. Mix in the egg replacer, then fold in the flour, ground almonds, baking powder, and xanthan gum. Fold in the golden raisins, along with any remaining liquid. Spoon the batter into the prepared pan and smooth the top with a spatula.

4 Bake in the preheated oven for 20–25 minutes, or until golden and springy to the touch. Sprinkle with the toasted slivered almonds and let cool in the pan for 10 minutes. Transfer to a wire rack to cool completely before slicing and serving with ice cream and a drizzle of maple syrup, if desired.

¼ cup golden raisins

1 tablespoon vegan amaretto

vegan and gluten-free egg replacer, equivalent to 4 eggs

½ cup firmly packed vegan and gluten-free margarine, plus extra for greasing

½ cup vegan superfine or granulated sugar

⅓ cup gluten-free all-purpose flour

1 cup ground almonds

1¼ teaspoons gluten-free baking powder

½ teaspoon xanthan gum

1 tablespoon toasted slivered almonds

vegan and gluten-free ice cream and maple syrup, to serve (optional)

Apricot & Apple
SPICED LOAF

A slice of this fruity loaf is perfect when spread with your favorite nondairy butter or vegan cream cheese.

1 Preheat the oven to 325°F. Grease a 9 x 5 x 3-inch loaf pan and line with parchment paper.

2 Place the dried apricot and apple into a small mixing bowl with the golden raisins. Add the cinnamon and allspice and stir together. Make up the egg replacer in a small bowl according to the package directions, and beat it with a fork for a minute, until bubbly.

3 Put the vegan margarine and sugar into a large mixing bowl and beat together with a wooden spoon until creamy. Beat in the egg replacer. Gradually stir in the flours, baking powder, and xanthan gum. Add enough of the soy milk to moisten the mixture—it should drop off a spoon easily.

4 Fold in the spiced dried fruits and spoon the batter into the prepared loaf pan. Smooth the top with a spatula.

5 Bake in the preheated oven for 1¼–1½ hours, or until golden brown and firm to the touch. Let the loaf cool in the pan for 10 minutes before turning it out onto a wire rack to cool completely.

¾ cup diced dried unwaxed apricots

⅓ cup diced dried unwaxed apples

3 tablespoons golden raisins

1 teaspoon ground cinnamon

1 teaspoon ground allspice

vegan and gluten-free egg replacer, equivalent to 2 eggs

½ cup firmly packed vegan and gluten-free margarine, plus extra for greasing

½ cup firmly packed vegan brown sugar

1 cup gluten-free all-purpose flour

⅓ cup rice flour

2½ teaspoons gluten-free baking powder

½ teaspoon xanthan gum

¼ cup gluten-free soy milk

Fresh Fruit LAYER CAKE

This is a showstopping layer cake that is perfect for a summer celebration. The maple-cashew nut filling is subtle, so the fruit flavors shine through.

3¼ cups gluten-free all-purpose flour

1 cup vegan granulated sugar

5 teaspoons gluten-free baking powder

1⅔ cups gluten-free soy milk

⅔ cup canola oil, plus extra for greasing

2 tablespoons vanilla extract

1 pound fresh seasonal unwaxed fruit, chopped (about 4 cups)

vegan and gluten-free confectioners' sugar, to decorate

MAPLE-CASHEW NUT FILLING

1⅔ cups cashew nuts

12 ounces extra firm silken tofu

3 tablespoons maple syrup

1 tablespoon canola oil

1 teaspoon vanilla extract

1 Preheat the oven to 350°F. Grease two 8-inch cake pans and line with parchment paper.

2 Put the flour, sugar, and baking powder into a large mixing bowl and stir together with a wooden spoon. Add the soy milk, oil, and vanilla, stir quickly to combine the wet and dry ingredients, and then spoon the batter into the prepared pans and smooth the tops with a rubber spatula. Bake in the preheated oven for 20 minutes, or until a toothpick inserted into the cakes comes out clean. Turn the cakes out onto a wire rack and let cool completely.

3 To make the filling, put the cashew nuts into a food processor and process them to a fine powder. Add the tofu, maple syrup, oil, and vanilla and process to a thick cream.

4 Carefully slice each cake in half to make four layers. Put one piece of cake onto a serving plate and build up the cake with layers of cashew cream and fresh fruit. Sift a little confectioners' sugar over the top of the cake and then pile some fresh fruit on top before serving.

Raspberry Chocolate CAKE

This is a deliciously decadent-looking cake, with a rich chocolate icing on top and fresh, zingy raspberries.

vegan and gluten-free margarine,
   for greasing

2⅓ cups gluten-free all-purpose flour

⅔ cup vegan and gluten-free
   unsweetened cocoa powder

½ teaspoon xanthan gum

1 teaspoon gluten-free baking powder

1 teaspoon gluten-free baking soda

½ teaspoon salt

1½ cups vegan granulated sugar

1½ cups gluten-free soy milk

½ cup canola oil

½ cup gluten-free seedless
   raspberry jelly or preserves

1 teaspoon vanilla extract

ICING

3 tablespoons gluten-free soy milk

3 ounces vegan and gluten-free
   semisweet chocolate, broken into
   small pieces

½ cup vegan and gluten-free
   confectioners' sugar

1 tablespoon maple syrup

fresh raspberries, to decorate

1 Preheat the oven to 350°F. Grease a 9-inch round cake pan and line with parchment paper.

2 Sift the flour, cocoa, xanthan gum, baking powder, and baking soda into a large mixing bowl and stir in the salt and sugar. Pour the soy milk into a medium saucepan and add the oil, raspberry jelly, and vanilla extract. Place over medium heat and whisk to combine. Stir into the dry ingredients and mix thoroughly.

3 Transfer to the prepared cake pan and bake in the preheated oven for 45 minutes, or until a toothpick inserted into the center comes out clean. Turn out and let cool completely on a wire rack before icing.

4 To make the icing, heat the soy milk in a small saucepan over medium heat until it reaches boiling point, then drop the chocolate into the pan and stir until completely melted. Remove from the heat and whisk in the confectioners' sugar and maple syrup. Set aside to cool before icing the cake, using a spatula. Top with a few fresh raspberries before slicing and serving.

Cook's tip

Substitute unwaxed, gluten-free orange marmalade for the raspberry preserves and decorate with sliced unwaxed oranges dipped in melted vegan and gluten-free chocolate.

3

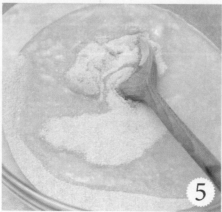
5

6

Blueberry POLENTA CAKE

Grated apple makes this cake sweet and moist and will have you coming back for seconds. Polenta is an Italian-style cornmeal available in most larger food stores.

1 Preheat the oven to 350°F. Grease an 8-inch round, loose-bottom cake pan and line with parchment paper.

2 Put the polenta, baking powder, and xanthan gum into a large mixing bowl and mix together thoroughly with a wooden spoon.

3 Make up the egg replacer in a small bowl according to the package directions, and beat it with a fork for a minute, until bubbly. Put the sugar and oil into a separate mixing bowl and beat together with a fork. Gradually add the egg replacer and lemon zest and continue to beat until the ingredients are well combined.

4 Peel, core, and grate the apple and mix into the wet ingredients with a wooden spoon.

5 Pour the wet ingredients onto the polenta mixture and stir well with a wooden spoon to combine.

6 Spoon the batter into the prepared cake pan and smooth the top with the back of a spoon. Sprinkle the blueberries on top of the cake and gently press them onto the surface of the batter.

7 Bake in the preheated oven for 35–40 minutes, or until golden and cooked through. Let the cake cool completely before removing from the pan.

vegan and gluten-free margarine, for greasing

1½ cups instant polenta

1 tablespoon gluten-free baking powder

1 teaspoon xanthan gum

vegan and gluten-free egg replacer, equivalent to 3 eggs

1 cup vegan superfine or granulated sugar

½ cup canola oil

zest of 1 unwaxed lemon

1 unwaxed apple

1 cup blueberries

Cook's tip
Choose a light canola oil that will not affect the flavor of the cake.

Carrot & Walnut
CAKE

It's easy to make a delicious carrot cake with vegan cream cheese—just try not to eat it before the cake is cool enough to frost.

1 Preheat the oven to 325°F. Grease a 7-inch round, loose-bottom cake pan and line with parchment paper.

2 Sift the flour and baking powder into a large mixing bowl. Stir in the sugar, cinnamon, nutmeg, and walnuts and mix well with a wooden spoon.

3 Stir the carrots into the dry ingredients, along with the maple syrup and canola oil, and mix well with a wooden spoon.

4 Spoon the batter into the prepared cake pan, smooth the top with a rubber spatula, and bake in the preheated oven for about 1 hour, or until a toothpick inserted into the center of the cake comes out clean. Let the cake cool in the pan for 10 minutes, until firm enough to handle, then transfer to a wire rack and let cool completely before frosting.

5 To make the frosting, beat together the cream cheese, margarine, and confectioners' sugar until smooth. Using an electric mixer is easiest for this, but you can do it with a fork, if necessary. Spread the filling generously on the top of the cake, and on the sides, too, if desired, and swirl the surface into an attractive pattern with a fork. Let set before serving.

vegan and gluten-free margarine, for greasing

1¾ cups gluten-free all-purpose flour

3¾ teaspoons gluten-free baking powder

½ cup firmly packed vegan brown sugar

2 teaspoons ground cinnamon

1 teaspoon ground nutmeg

⅔ cup coarsely chopped walnuts

2 cups shredded carrots

½ cup maple syrup

½ cup canola oil

CREAM CHEESE FROSTING

½ cup vegan and gluten-free cream cheese

¼ cup firmly packed vegan and gluten-free margarine

1¾ cups vegan and gluten-free confectioners' sugar

Cook's tip

To make a layer cake, carefully slice the cake in half and sandwich with the cream cheese frosting. Using two cake pans tends to make the cake dry and hard around the edges.

Cook's tip

This cake would also be great served as a dessert, with vegan and gluten-free ice cream.

Mixed Berry
BUNDT CAKE

This cake is bursting with fresh summer flavors, with raspberries, blueberries, and blackberries, as well as coconut.

1 Preheat the oven to 350°F. Grease and flour a 9½-inch bundt pan.

2 Sift together the flour, xanthan gum, baking powder, and baking soda into a large bowl and stir in the sugar and coconut. Add the soy milk, oil, and vanilla extract. Beat together until smooth and a thick batter. Stir in the salt and berries.

3 Pour the batter into the prepared bundt pan. Bake in the preheated oven for 1 hour, or until a toothpick inserted into the cake comes out clean. Let cool in the pan for 5 minutes before turning out onto a wire rack.

4 When the cake has cooled, dust it with confectioners' sugar and fill the center with more fresh berries. Slice and serve.

2¾ cups gluten-free all-purpose flour, plus extra for dusting

½ teaspoon xanthan gum

2 teaspoons gluten-free baking powder

1 teaspoon gluten-free baking soda

2 cups vegan superfine or granulated sugar

¾ cup dry unsweetened coconut

2 cups gluten-free soy milk

⅔ cup canola oil, plus extra for greasing

2 teaspoons vanilla extract

1 teaspoon salt

2 cups mixed berries, such as raspberries, blueberries, and blackberries, plus extra to serve

vegan and gluten-free confectioners' sugar, to dust

PREP TIME: 20 minutes COOK TIME: 25–30 minutes SERVES: 8

Fig Upside-Down CAKE

What better way to enjoy the beautiful color of fresh figs than by using them in an upside-down cake?

- vegan and gluten-free margarine, for greasing
- 3 tablespoons packed vegan light brown sugar
- 4 fresh, unwaxed figs, halved vertically
- zest of 1 unwaxed orange
- 1⅔ cups gluten-free all-purpose flour
- ½ cup vegan granulated sugar
- 2½ teaspoons gluten-free baking powder
- 1 teaspoon ground cinnamon
- 1 cup gluten-free soy milk
- ⅓ cup canola oil

1 Preheat the oven to 350°F. Grease an 8-inch round cake pan and line with parchment paper.

2 Sprinkle the brown sugar into the bottom of the prepared pan. Arrange the figs on top of the sugar in the pan, cut side down. Sprinkle the orange zest over the figs.

3 Put the flour into a large mixing bowl and stir in the granulated sugar, baking powder, and cinnamon.

4 Mix the soy milk and oil together in a small bowl. Pour the wet ingredients over the dry ingredients and mix together quickly, with a rubber spatula, until just combined. Spoon the batter into the pan, carefully covering the figs, and smooth the top.

5 Bake in the preheated oven for 25–30 minutes, or until a toothpick inserted into the center of the cake comes out clean. Let the cake cool in the pan for 5 minutes, then turn it out onto a serving plate. This cake is best served warm.

Cook's tip

Turn the cake out onto a serving plate, not a wire rack, so that you catch any juices from the fig topping. These juices can then be drizzled back over the cake.

Pear & Pecan CAKE

A topping of oven-roasted pears makes this a moist cake and the pecans add a pleasant nutty texture.

1 Preheat the oven to 350°F. Grease a 9-inch round, loose-bottom cake pan.

2 Divide the pecans into two equal portions. Chop one portion very finely. Put the finely chopped pecans into the prepared cake pan and tip the pan so that the chopped nuts stick to the greased bottom and sides of the pan. Tip out any spare nuts onto a plate.

3 Put the flour, sugar, and baking powder into a large mixing bowl and stir together. Chop the remaining pecans coarsely and stir them into the dry ingredients along with any of the leftover finely chopped pecans.

4 Put the soy milk into a small bowl and add the oil, maple syrup, and vanilla extract.

5 Pour the wet ingredients into the bowl of dry ingredients and quickly mix with a wooden spoon until just combined. Spoon the batter into the prepared pan and smooth the surface with a spatula. Bake in the preheated oven for 35–40 minutes, or until firm and golden. Let the cake cool in the pan for 10 minutes, then turn it out onto a wire rack to cool. Leave the oven on.

6 To make the topping, place the pears in the bottom of a large baking dish. Sprinkle with the sugar and lemon juice and dot with margarine. Bake for 30 minutes, basting every 10 minutes, then set aside to cool.

7 Decorate the cake by overlapping the pear slices in a circle around the edge and then fill the gap in the center with pecan halves.

vegan and gluten-free margarine, for greasing

1 cup pecans

1⅔ cups gluten-free all-purpose flour

½ cup vegan granulated sugar

2½ teaspoons gluten-free baking powder

1 cup gluten-free soy milk

⅓ cup canola oil

2 tablespoons maple syrup

1 teaspoon vanilla extract

TOPPING

2 unwaxed Bosc pears, halved, cored, and sliced

2 tablespoons vegan superfine or granulated sugar

juice of ½ an unwaxed lemon

2 tablespoons packed vegan and gluten-free margarine

¼ cup pecan halves

Strawberry RED VELVET CAKE

This spectacular cake owes its rich, red color to beet, but tastes of raspberries and strawberries.

2 raw beets

1½ cups raspberries

vegan and gluten-free egg replacer, equivalent to 4 eggs

1 cup gluten-free soy milk

2 tablespoons vegan and gluten-free cider vinegar

2¼ cups gluten-free all-purpose flour

3 tablespoons vegan and gluten-free unsweetened cocoa powder

1 teaspoon xanthan gum

4 teaspoons gluten-free baking powder

1 teaspoon gluten-free cream of tartar

¾ cup firmly packed vegan and gluten-free margarine, plus extra for greasing

2¼ cups vegan granulated sugar

1 teaspoon vanilla extract

FILLING

2 tablespoons packed vegan and gluten-free margarine

2 tablespoons packed vegetable shortening

¼ cup vegan and gluten-free cream cheese

3 cups vegan and gluten-free confectioners' sugar, plus extra for dusting

1 teaspoon vanilla extract

2–3 tablespoons gluten-free soy milk

2 tablespoons freeze-dried strawberry pieces

1 cup fresh strawberries

1 Trim, peel, and grate the beets and put them into the bowl of a food processor with the raspberries. Process until smooth.

2 Preheat the oven to 350°F. Grease two 8-inch cake pans and line with parchment paper. Make up the egg replacer in a small bowl according to the package directions, and beat it with a fork for a minute, until bubbly.

3 Put the soy milk into a small bowl, stir in the vinegar, and set aside to curdle. Put the flour, cocoa powder, xanthan gum, baking powder, and cream of tartar into a large mixing bowl and stir together with a wooden spoon. In a separate bowl, cream the margarine and sugar together and beat in the egg replacer and vanilla extract.

4 Stir the milk mixture and the margarine mixture into the dry ingredients and mix thoroughly. Pour in the beet and raspberry puree and stir together with a wooden spoon until the batter is thoroughly combined.

5 Spoon the batter into the prepared pans and smooth the tops with a spatula. Bake in the preheated oven for 25–30 minutes, or until a toothpick inserted into the cakes comes out clean. Turn out onto a wire rack and let cool completely.

6 To make the filling, beat the margarine, vegetable shortening, and cream cheese together with the confectioners' sugar and vanilla. It's easiest to use an electric mixer, but you can do it in a large mixing bowl with a fork. Add a little soy milk, if necessary. When the mixture is smooth, stir in the freeze-dried strawberry pieces.

7 Spread the bottom layer of the cake with the filling. Cut the fresh strawberries in half and arrange them over the layer of filling, pressing them in. Sandwich with the second layer of the cake and dust with confectioners' sugar to serve.

Cook's tip

The raspberries cover any beet taste in this cake. They also create an acidic mixture that helps prevent the beet from browning as it bakes.

Vegan Ricotta CAKE

A contradiction in terms? A vegan "ricotta" made with cashew nuts and dates works perfectly in this cake.

1 To make the ricotta, soak the cashew nuts in ½ cup of water for about 30 minutes. Put the dates into the bowl of a food processor along with the cashews and the soaking water. Process to a thick, smooth consistency.

2 Preheat the oven to 350°F. Grease a 9-inch square baking pan and line with parchment paper. Make up the egg replacer in a small bowl according to the package directions, and beat it with a fork for a minute, until bubbly.

3 In a large mixing bowl, cream the margarine and sugar together with a wooden spoon. Beat in the vegan ricotta and egg replacer. Add in the flour, baking powder, xanthan gum, and coffee powder and mix thoroughly.

4 Spoon the batter into the prepared pan and smooth the top with a spatula. Bake in the preheated oven for 30 minutes, or until golden and springy to the touch. Let cool in the pan for 5 minutes before transferring to a wire rack to cool completely.

VEGAN RICOTTA

⅔ cup raw cashew nuts

¼ cup coarsely chopped, pitted unwaxed dates

vegan and gluten-free egg replacer, equivalent to 2 eggs

½ cup firmly packed vegan and gluten-free margarine, plus extra for greasing

1 cup vegan superfine or granulated sugar

1⅔ cups gluten-free all-purpose flour

2 teaspoons gluten-free baking powder

1 teaspoon xanthan gum

2 teaspoons instant coffee powder

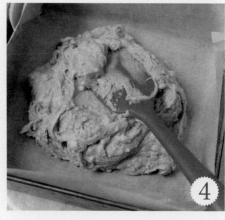

Chocolate Mint MARBLE CAKE

This is a fun-looking cake with swirls of chocolate and crunchy green sugar sprinkles that would be good for serving at a teenager's party.

1 Preheat the oven to 350°F. Grease a 9-inch round, loose-bottom cake pan.

2 Put the flour, sugar, and baking powder into a large mixing bowl and stir together with a wooden spoon.

3 Put the soy milk into a small bowl and add the oil.

4 Pour the wet ingredients into the bowl of dry ingredients and quickly mix with a wooden spoon until just combined. Spoon half of the batter into another mixing bowl.

5 Add the cocoa to one bowl and the peppermint extract and green food coloring to the other. Mix each quickly to combine, then spoon the batters into the prepared pan. Use a knife to swirl through the batters, and smooth the surface with a spatula. Bake in the preheated oven for 25–30 minutes, or until firm and golden. Let the cake cool in the pan for 10 minutes, then turn it out onto a wire rack to cool before decorating.

6 To make the topping, melt the semisweet chocolate with the soy cream in a microwave in short 30-second bursts, or alternatively melt together in a double boiler or a heatproof bowl set over a saucepan of gently simmering water. Put the granulated sugar into a bowl and mix in the peppermint extract and green food coloring. Drizzle the melted chocolate over the cake, then sprinkle the peppermint sugar over the top. Let the chocolate cool and set before serving.

1¾ cups gluten-free all-purpose flour

½ cup vegan granulated sugar

3¼ teaspoons gluten-free baking powder

1 cup gluten-free soy milk

⅓ cup canola oil, plus extra for greasing

¼ cup vegan and gluten-free unsweetened cocoa powder

½ teaspoon peppermint extract

½ teaspoon green food coloring

TOPPING

2 ounces vegan and gluten-free semisweet chocolate, broken into pieces

1 tablespoon gluten-free soy cream

2 tablespoons vegan granulated sugar

½ teaspoon peppermint extract

¼ teaspoon green food coloring

Cook's tip

You can make your own vegan after-dinner mints by stirring this peppermint sugar into melted chocolate and spooning it onto a silicone baking sheet to set.

4

5

6

Cook's tip

Black or red cherries work well visually with this cake. Be sure to use the best-quality cherry preserves you can find— homemade would be perfect.

Cherry & Vanilla BUNDT CAKE

Filled with luscious ripe cherries, this cake makes a beautiful centerpiece for a summer afternoon get-together.

1 Preheat the oven to 350°F. Grease a 9½-inch bundt pan.

2 Put the flour, sugar, and baking powder into a large mixing bowl and stir together with a wooden spoon.

3 Put the soy milk into a small bowl and add the oil and vanilla extract. Stir in 3 tablespoons of cherry preserves. Set aside 5 tablespoons of cherry preserves to use to decorate the cake once it is baked.

4 Pour the wet ingredients into the bowl of dry ingredients and quickly mix with a wooden spoon until just combined. Spoon half of the batter into the prepared pan. Dot the surface of the cake batter with teaspoonfuls of the remaining ½ cup of cherry preserves. Cover with the rest of the cake batter. Bake for 30–35 minutes, or until firm and golden. Let the cake cool in the pan for 10 minutes, then turn out onto a wire rack to cool.

5 Put the reserved preserves into a small saucepan with 1 tablespoon of water and heat gently to melt into a runny syrup. Strain the syrup through a strainer, discard the solids, and set the syrup aside to cool.

6 When the cake is cool, transfer it to a serving plate and fill the hole in the center with fresh cherries. Drizzle the cake and the fresh cherries with the cherry syrup just before serving.

2⅓ cups gluten-free all-purpose flour

1 cup vegan granulated sugar

3¾ teaspoons gluten-free baking powder

1¼ cups gluten-free soy milk

½ cup canola oil, plus extra for greasing

1 tablespoon vanilla extract

1 cup gluten-free, unwaxed cherry preserves

2 cups fresh, unwaxed cherries

Chocolate Fudge CAKE

The texture of this cake is like a brownie—soft inside, with a slightly crispy edge and a cracked surface that hints at the fudgy chocolate delights within.

4 ounces vegan and gluten-free semisweet chocolate, broken into pieces

½ cup firmly packed vegan and gluten-free margarine, plus extra for greasing

1½ cups vegan superfine or granulated sugar

1 teaspoon vegan glycerin

½ teaspoon vanilla extract

vegan and gluten-free egg replacer, equivalent to 2 eggs

½ cup gluten-free soy cream

¾ cup rice flour

¾ cup gluten-free all-purpose flour

½ teaspoon xanthan gum

1¼ teaspoons gluten-free baking powder

½ teaspoon gluten-free baking soda

FROSTING

6 ounces vegan and gluten-free semisweet chocolate, broken into pieces

⅔ cup gluten-free soy cream

1⅔ cups vegan and gluten-free confectioners' sugar, plus extra to decorate

½ cup firmly packed vegan and gluten-free margarine

1 Preheat the oven to 350°F. Grease two 8-inch cake pans and line with parchment paper.

2 Put the chocolate into the top of a double boiler or in a small heatproof bowl set over a saucepan of gently simmering water. Heat gently until the chocolate is melted and then set aside to cool.

3 In a large mixing bowl, cream together the margarine, sugar, glycerin, and vanilla. Make up the egg replacer in a small bowl according to the package directions, and beat it with a fork for a minute, until bubbly. Add the egg replacer to the mixing bowl and beat until it is light and fluffy. Stir in the soy cream and the cooled chocolate. Fold in the rice flour, all-purpose flour, xanthan gum, baking powder, and baking soda.

4 Spoon the batter into the prepared pans and smooth the tops with a rubber spatula. Bake in the preheated oven for 30 minutes, or until a toothpick inserted into the cakes comes out clean. Let cool in the pans for 30 minutes, then turn them out onto a wire rack. Let cool completely.

5 To make the frosting, put the chocolate and soy cream into a small double boiler or a heatproof bowl set over a saucepan of gently simmering water. Heat gently, stirring, until the chocolate is melted and then set aside to cool.

6 Cream the confectioners' sugar and margarine together in a small bowl, then pour in the cooled chocolate mixture. Beat well for 2–3 minutes, or until it thickens to a fudgelike consistency.

7 Sandwich the cakes together with the frosting and sift a little confectioners' sugar over the top of the cake before serving.

Cook's tip

For any serious chocoholics, you could always double the quantities of frosting and cover the top and sides of the cake for a truly decadent treat.

4

5

7

Orange Olive Oil CAKE

This moist cake is rich with Mediterranean flavors to bring some sunshine to your table whatever the time of year!

1 Preheat the oven to 350°F. Grease a 9-inch round, springform cake pan and line with parchment paper.

2 Put the pine nuts into a heavy saucepan and warm gently over low heat, stirring constantly with a wooden spatula until they begin to turn golden. Transfer to a plate and set aside.

3 Sift the flour, xanthan gum, and baking powder into a large mixing bowl. Stir in the ground almonds, superfine sugar, and orange zest.

4 Make up the egg replacer in a small bowl according to the package directions, and beat it with a fork for a minute, until bubbly.

5 Add the almond milk, olive oil, and coconut oil to the dry ingredients and mix well. Fold in the egg replacer with a rubber spatula. Finally, stir in the orange juice and toasted pine nuts.

6 Spoon the batter into the prepared cake pan and smooth the top with a rubber spatula. Bake in the preheated oven for 40 minutes, or until a toothpick inserted into the cake comes out clean. Release the sides of the cake pan and transfer the cake to a wire rack to cool.

7 To make the orange slices, cut the orange into circles about ¼ inch thick and halve each circle. Put the sugar into a heavy saucepan with 1½ cups of water and bring to a boil, stirring frequently to be sure the sugar dissolves. Add the orange slices and simmer over medium heat for about 20 minutes, turning the oranges occasionally, until the sugar water has reduced to a thin syrup. Reduce the heat and continue to cook for an additional 10 minutes, until the syrup is thick. Transfer the oranges to a wire rack to cool.

8 Prick the cake with a toothpick and slowly pour over the warm orange syrup. When the orange slices are cool, arrange them in a decorative pattern on top of the cake.

1⅔ cups pine nuts

1⅓ cups gluten-free all-purpose flour

1 teaspoon xanthan gum

2 teaspoons gluten-free baking powder

½ cup ground almonds

1 cup vegan superfine or granulated sugar

zest and juice of 1 unwaxed orange

vegan and gluten-free egg replacer, equivalent to 4 eggs

⅓ cup almond milk

⅔ cup extra virgin olive oil, plus extra for greasing

⅓ cup coconut oil

CRYSTALLIZED ORANGE SLICES

1 large unwaxed orange, scrubbed

½ cup vegan granulated sugar

Cook's tip

For a quicker alternative to the orange slices, pour 2 tablespoons vegan orange liqueur over the cake, let it cool, and dust with vegan and gluten-free confectioners' sugar.

CHAPTER 2
Small Cakes

Cookies & Cream CUPCAKES

Perhaps it's the unexpected crunch inside these cupcakes that makes them such a firm family favorite!

2 cups gluten-free soy milk

1 teaspoon vegan and gluten-free cider vinegar

¾ cup vegan superfine or granulated sugar

⅓ cup canola oil

1 teaspoon vanilla extract

1¼ cups gluten-free all-purpose flour

¼ cup vegan and gluten-free unsweetened cocoa powder

¾ teaspoon gluten-free baking soda

½ teaspoon gluten-free baking powder

⅔ cup crushed vegan and gluten-free cookies (see tip on right)

TOPPING

2½ tablespoons packed vegan and gluten-free margarine

3 tablespoons packed vegetable shortening

2⅓ cups vegan and gluten-free confectioners' sugar

¾ teaspoon vanilla extract

⅓ cup gluten-free soy cream

⅓ cup crushed vegan and gluten-free cookies

1 Preheat the oven to 350°F. Line a 12-section cupcake pan with paper liners.

2 Put the soy milk into a small bowl, stir in the vinegar, and set aside for a few minutes to curdle.

3 Put the sugar, oil, and vanilla into a large mixing bowl and beat together. Pour in the milk and vinegar, mix thoroughly, and then add the flour, cocoa powder, baking soda, and baking powder. Stir until the ingredients are just combined, then fold in the cookie crumbs.

4 Divide the batter evenly among the paper liners and bake in the preheated oven for 18–20 minutes, or until springy to the touch and golden. Transfer to a wire rack to cool completely before frosting.

5 To make the topping, beat together the margarine and vegetable shortening, then mix in the confectioners' sugar and the vanilla. Gradually add the soy cream to achieve a thick piping consistency. Pipe or spoon the frosting generously over the cupcakes and sprinkle with the cookie crumbs.

Cook's tip

If you are unsure of which
cookies to use, the chocolate
cookies used to make the
Ice Cream Sandwiches on
page 100 would work
well in this recipe.

Pink Champagne CUPCAKES

Celebration cupcakes that aren't too sweet—and they taste just delicious with a glass of pink champagne.

1 Preheat the oven to 350°F. Line a 12-section cupcake pan with paper liners.

2 Put the soy milk into a small bowl, stir in the vinegar, and set aside for a few minutes to curdle.

3 Put the sugar, oil, and vanilla into a large mixing bowl and beat together. Pour in the milk and vinegar and the wine and mix thoroughly. Add the flour, baking soda, baking powder, and salt and mix thoroughly. Finally, fold in the strawberry pieces.

4 Divide the batter evenly among the paper liners. Bake in the preheated oven for 18–20 minutes, or until springy to the touch and golden. Transfer to a wire rack to cool completely.

5 To make the topping, beat the margarine, vegetable shortening, and 4 cups of the confectioners' sugar together. Add the wine and jelly or preserves. Mix well and beat in enough additional confectioners' sugar to achieve a piping consistency. Pipe generous swirls of frosting onto the cakes and decorate with a sprinkling of freeze-dried strawberry pieces.

⅓ cup gluten-free soy milk

1 teaspoon vegan and gluten-free cider vinegar

2 tablespoons vegan superfine or granulated sugar

¼ cup canola oil

½ teaspoon vanilla extract

⅓ cup vegan sparkling rosé wine

1 cup gluten-free all-purpose flour

½ teaspoon gluten-free baking soda

½ teaspoon gluten-free baking powder

½ teaspoon salt

1 tablespoon freeze-dried strawberry pieces

TOPPING

¼ cup firmly packed vegan and gluten-free margarine

¼ cup firmly packed vegetable shortening

5¼ cups vegan and gluten-free confectioners' sugar

¼ cup vegan sparkling rosé wine

1 tablespoon gluten-free strawberry jelly or preserves

freeze-dried strawberry pieces, to decorate

Cook's tip

If you don't have coffee extract, you could always mix a teaspoon of instant coffee granules with two teaspoons of cold water and use this mixture instead.

Coffee & Salted Caramel
CUPCAKES

If you're baking to impress, these stunning cupcakes are the perfect showcase for your talents.

1 Preheat the oven to 350°F. Line a 12-section cupcake pan with paper liners.

2 Put the flour, superfine sugar, and baking powder into a large mixing bowl and stir together with a wooden spoon. Stir the soy milk, canola oil, and coffee extract into the dry ingredients. Divide the batter among the paper liners and bake in the preheated oven for 15–20 minutes, or until a toothpick inserted comes out clean. Transfer to a wire rack to cool. When the cakes are cool, use a melon baller or a teaspoon to scoop out a circular well in the top of each one. Discard the scooped-out cake pieces.

3 To make the sugar shards, if using, cover a baking sheet with aluminum foil. Sprinkle the hazelnuts and salt over the foil. Put the superfine sugar into a small saucepan with ½ cup of cold water and heat gently, stirring frequently, until the sugar is completely dissolved. Increase the heat and bring the mixture to a boil, then keep it on a gentle boil, stirring continuously, for 5 minutes, or until it is syrupy. Carefully pour the syrup over the nuts and salt to make a thin layer and set aside to cool. When completely cool, carefully peel the foil off the sugar and use a sharp knife to break the sugar into shards.

4 To make the caramel, put the sugar, agave nectar, margarine, and coconut cream into a saucepan and heat gently to melt the ingredients together. Keep stirring the mixture until the sugar dissolves, then increase the temperature and gradually bring the mixture to 235°F—"soft ball" stage. If you don't have a candy thermometer, you can test the caramel by chilling a plate in the refrigerator for a few minutes, then putting a blob of caramel onto it. If it immediately forms a skin and holds its shape, it's ready. Take it off the heat and stir in the vanilla extract and salt.

5 Spoon the warm caramel into the wells in the cupcakes, being careful to avoid overfilling them. Place a sugar shard into the caramel on each cake while it is still warm. Set the cakes aside to cool. If including the sugar shards, serve the cupcakes within the hour; the sugar shards will begin to dissolve if the cakes are left for longer.

1¼ cups gluten-free all-purpose flour

⅓ cup vegan superfine or granulated sugar

1¾ teaspoons gluten-free baking powder

⅔ cup gluten-free soy milk

¼ cup canola oil

2 teaspoons gluten-free coffee extract

SALTED SUGAR SHARDS (OPTIONAL)

3 tablespoons roasted hazelnuts, chopped

¼ teaspoon sea salt

½ cup vegan superfine or granulated sugar

SALTED CARAMEL

½ cup vegan superfine or granulated sugar

¼ cup agave nectar

2 tablespoons packed vegan and gluten-free margarine

⅓ cup coconut cream

½ teaspoon vanilla extract

¼ teaspoon sea salt

Green Tea CUPCAKES

A subtle green tea flavor makes these eye-catching cakes perfect to serve at the end of an Eastern-style banquet.

1 Preheat the oven to 350°F. Line a 12-section muffin pan with paper liners.

2 Make up the egg replacer in a small bowl according to the package directions, and beat it with a fork for a minute, until bubbly. Put the sugar and egg replacer into a mixing bowl and, using an electric mixer, beat on high speed for a minute, until frothy.

3 Sift the flour, baking powder, and xanthan gum into a large mixing bowl. Add the sugar mixture and stir in the matcha green tea powder.

4 Put the oil and rice milk into a small bowl and stir with a metal spoon. Pour over the flour mixture and mix thoroughly.

5 Divide the batter equally among the paper liners and bake in the preheated oven for 25 minutes, or until a toothpick inserted into the center of a cupcake comes out clean. Transfer to a wire rack to cool completely before frosting.

6 To make the frosting, put the margarine, vegetable shortening, matcha green tea powder, and confectioners' sugar in a large mixing bowl and cream together. A handheld electric mixer is easiest for this, but it can also be done with a fork. Gradually beat in the rice milk until firm. Spoon the frosting into a pastry bag. Decorate each cupcake with a generous swirl of frosting and a sprinkle of pistachios.

vegan and gluten-free egg replacer, equivalent to 2 eggs

1 cup vegan superfine or granulated sugar

1⅓ cups gluten-free all-purpose flour

2¾ teaspoons gluten-free baking powder

½ teaspoon xanthan gum

4 teaspoons matcha green tea powder

½ cup canola oil

½ cup rice milk

FROSTING

⅓ cup firmly packed vegan and gluten-free margarine

⅓ cup firmly packed vegetable shortening

2 teaspoons matcha green tea powder

4¾ cups vegan and gluten-free confectioners' sugar

¼ cup rice milk

3 tablespoons shelled finely chopped pistachio nuts

Raspberry & Dark Chocolate
CUPCAKES

These pretty cupcakes have a combination of thick, rich chocolate and shocking pink sprinkles that makes them perfect for a girls' night in.

vegan and gluten-free egg replacer, equivalent to 2 eggs

1 cup vegan superfine or granulated sugar

1 teaspoon vegan glycerin

1¼ cups gluten-free all-purpose flour

2¼ teaspoons gluten-free baking powder

½ teaspoon xanthan gum

⅓ cup ground almonds

2 ounces vegan and gluten-free semisweet chocolate, chopped

½ cup canola oil

¼ cup gluten-free soy milk

¼ cup gluten-free soy cream

2 tablespoons gluten-free raspberry jelly or preserves

chopped freeze-dried raspberries, to decorate (optional)

CHOCOLATE TOPPING

2 ounces vegan and gluten-free semisweet chocolate, broken into pieces

2 tablespoons gluten-free soy cream

½ teaspoon vanilla extract

1 Preheat the oven to 350°F. Line a 12-section cupcake pan with paper liners. Make up the egg replacer in a small bowl according to the package directions, and beat it with a fork for a minute, until bubbly.

2 Put the sugar, glycerin, and egg replacer into a large mixing bowl and, using an electric mixer, beat on high speed for a minute, until frothy.

3 Sift the flour, baking powder, and xanthan gum into the sugar mixture. Stir in the ground almonds and the chocolate.

4 Put the oil, soy milk, and soy cream into a small bowl and stir with a metal spoon. Pour over the flour mixture and mix thoroughly.

5 Put a little batter into each paper liner and use the back of a teaspoon to spread it out over the bottom. Put half a teaspoon of raspberry jelly or preserves into each liner, then divide the remaining cupcake batter between the liners and smooth the tops with a spatula. Bake in the preheated oven for 20–25 minutes, or until springy to the touch and golden. Transfer to a wire rack to cool completely before icing.

6 To make the chocolate topping, place the chocolate into a double boiler or a heatproof bowl with the soy cream. Heat gently over a saucepan of gently simmering water to melt the chocolate. Stir frequently with a metal spoon to mix together the chocolate and soy cream. Stir in the vanilla extract. Remove the bowl from the heat and beat the mixture with a metal fork until glossy and smooth. Decorate each cupcake with a thick layer of chocolate and a sprinkle of dried raspberries, if using. Set aside to cool and firm before serving.

Cook's tip

Many cake decorations contain egg or shellac, which are not suitable for vegans. Dried blueberries make a pretty alternative topping for these cupcakes.

Blue Velvet CUPCAKES

Red velvet cupcakes often include beets—these unusual blue cakes contain ripe, buttery avocado for a rich, velvety texture.

1 Preheat the oven to 350°F. Line a 12-section miniature cupcake pan with paper liners.

2 Peel, pit, and mash the avocado until smooth. Place the avocado in a small bowl with the soy milk and vinegar, stir for a few seconds to combine the ingredients, and set aside to curdle.

3 Put the oil, vanilla, and food coloring paste into a small bowl and stir with a fork to combine.

4 In a large bowl, sift together the flour, xanthan gum, and baking powder and stir in the sugar with a wooden spoon.

5 Pour the soy milk mixture and the oil mixture onto the dry ingredients and stir well, making sure the blue coloring is well dispersed. While overstirring can result in rubbery cupcakes if using flour that contains gluten, in this recipe you can stir for as long as it takes to thoroughly combine the ingredients.

6 Divide the batter evenly among the paper liners. Bake in the preheated oven for 20–25 minutes, or until cooked through and springy to the touch. Transfer to a wire rack and let cool completely before frosting.

7 To make the frosting, beat the margarine and vegetable shortening together until soft and fluffy. An electric mixer is easiest for this, but if you don't have one, put the margarine and shortening into a large mixing bowl and beat together with a fork until fluffy and well combined. Beat in the confectioners' sugar and soy milk and as much blue food coloring as you need to achieve your desired effect. Pipe or spread the frosting generously onto the cupcakes.

½ ripe unwaxed avocado

1 cup gluten-free soy milk

4 teaspoons vegan and gluten-free cider vinegar

⅓ cup canola oil

1 teaspoon vanilla extract

1 teaspoon gluten-free blue food coloring paste

1⅔ cups gluten-free all-purpose flour

½ teaspoon xanthan gum

2 teaspoons gluten-free baking powder

1 cup vegan superfine or granulated sugar

FROSTING

⅓ cup firmly packed vegan and gluten-free margarine

⅓ cup firmly packed vegetable shortening

4¾ cups vegan and gluten-free confectioners' sugar

¼ cup gluten-free soy milk

¼–½ teaspoon gluten-free blue food coloring paste

Almond CUPCAKES

These simple almond cupcakes are enhanced by a delicious white chocolate icing.

1 Preheat the oven to 350°F. Line a cupcake pan with 10 paper liners.

2 Put the oil, yogurt, milk, sugar, almond extract, and ground almonds into a large mixing bowl. Sift in the flour, xanthan gum, baking powder, and salt, then beat with an electric mixer until the mixture is well combined.

3 Divide the batter among the liners in the prepared cupcake pan and bake in the preheated oven for 20–25 minutes, or until well risen and golden. Transfer the cupcakes to a wire rack and let cool completely before icing.

4 To make the icing, melt the chocolate in a double boiler or a large heatproof bowl set over a saucepan of simmering water. Remove from the heat and let cool slightly. Beat in the confectioners' sugar and soy milk. While the icing is still a little warm and easy to spread, spread it over the cupcakes with a teaspoon. Top each cupcake with a few toasted slivered almonds.

⅓ cup canola oil

¼ cup gluten-free soy yogurt

⅔ cup gluten-free soy milk

¾ cup vegan superfine or granulated sugar

3 tablespoons almond extract

⅓ cup ground almonds

1¼ cups gluten-free all-purpose flour

½ teaspoon xanthan gum

1½ teaspoons gluten-free baking powder

½ teaspoon salt

ICING

2 ounces vegan and gluten-free white chocolate, broken into pieces

¾ cup vegan and gluten-free confectioners' sugar

1½ tablespoons gluten-free soy milk

toasted slivered almonds, to decorate

Cook's tip
If you would like these cupcakes to look more special, replace the slivered almonds with gold candied balls.

Mojito CUPCAKES

These cupcakes are perfect for a hot summer afternoon, but be careful who gets one—these are strictly for the grown-ups.

1 cup gluten-free soy milk

2 sprigs fresh mint

1 teaspoon vegan and gluten-free cider vinegar

1 cup vegan superfine or granulated sugar

⅓ cup canola oil

1¼ cups gluten-free all-purpose flour

2 tablespoons gluten-free cornstarch

½ teaspoon gluten-free baking soda

½ teaspoon gluten-free baking powder

½ teaspoon salt

¼ cup vegan white rum

juice of 2 unwaxed limes

2 tablespoons packed vegan light brown sugar

TOPPING

½ cup firmly packed vegan and gluten-free margarine

¾ cup firmly packed vegetable shortening

5¼ cups vegan and gluten-free confectioners' sugar

fresh unwaxed lime slices and fresh mint sprigs, to decorate

1 Put the soy milk into a small saucepan with the mint. Bring to a boil, then remove from the heat and let cool before removing the mint.

2 Preheat the oven to 350°F and line a 12-section cupcake pan with paper liners.

3 Put the soy milk into a small bowl, stir in the vinegar, and set aside for a few minutes to curdle.

4 Put the sugar and oil into a large mixing bowl and beat together with a wooden spoon. Pour in the milk and vinegar and mix thoroughly. Add the flour, cornstarch, baking soda, baking powder, and salt and mix together thoroughly.

5 Divide the batter evenly among the paper liners. Bake in the preheated oven for 20 minutes, or until springy to the touch and golden.

6 Using a pastry brush, brush the tops of the cupcakes with some of the rum. Let it soak in and repeat two or three times. Brush with some of the lime juice and sprinkle each cake with a little brown sugar. Set aside the remaining rum and lime juice. Transfer the cupcakes to a wire rack to cool completely.

7 To make the topping, beat together the margarine, vegetable shortening, and 4 cups of the confectioners' sugar in a bowl until smooth. Beat in the remaining rum and lime juice. Gradually beat in additional confectioners' sugar until the frosting reaches a piping consistency. Pipe the frosting generously onto the cupcakes and decorate each with a piece of lime and a fresh mint sprig.

Cook's tip

Mint tea bags can also be used to steep the soy milk in step 1.

Cook's tip

It is best to use a grater for the orange zest in the icing, but you could also use a zesting tool or a sharp knife to cut the decorative zest strips for these cake pops.

Chocolate Orange CAKE POPS

*These fun, quirky-looking cake pops make a delicious contrast
to traditional chocolate-covered cake pops.*

1 Make the brownie cake according to the recipe on page 94, but without the macadamia nuts. Let cool completely. Crumble the brownie into a large mixing bowl.

2 To make the filling, beat the margarine and shortening together with a wooden spoon. Mix in the confectioners' sugar with enough soy cream to make a filling with a thick, spreadable consistency.

3 Add a little filling to the brownie crumbs and use your hands to mix it in. Gradually add more filling and use your hands to knead the mixture together. Continue to add the filling until the mixture can be squeezed into small balls that hold together. Cover the bowl with plastic wrap and refrigerate the mixture for 30 minutes.

4 Line a baking sheet with parchment paper. Roll the cake mixture into 24 small balls and place them on the prepared pan. Push a lollipop stick into each ball. Put the cake pops on the sheet and freeze for 30 minutes, until firm.

5 To make a pourable fondant icing, put the confectioners' sugar, corn syrup, orange juice, and grated orange zest into a saucepan over low heat and stir continuously until the icing is a pouring consistency but not too thin.

6 Take the cake pops out of the freezer and dip each one into the orange icing. Sprinkle with a few strips of orange zest. Return to the lined baking sheet and place in the freezer for 20 minutes, until firm.

1 chocolate brownie cake (see page 94), but made without macadamia nuts

24 lollipop sticks

FILLING

2 tablespoons packed vegan and gluten-free margarine

2 tablespoons packed vegetable shortening

1¾ cups vegan and gluten-free confectioners' sugar

¼ cup gluten-free soy cream

FONDANT ICING

6 cups vegan and gluten-free confectioners' sugar

2 tablespoons light corn syrup

¼ cup juice of 1 unwaxed orange

grated zest from 1 unwaxed orange, plus zest from 1 large unwaxed orange, cut into strips

Chocolate Coconut CAKE POPS

These fashionable bite-size treats are easy to make if you have a spare batch of brownies.

1 Make the brownie cake according to the recipe on page 94, but without the macadamia nuts. Let cool completely. Crumble the brownie into a large mixing bowl.

2 To make the filling, beat the margarine and shortening together with a wooden spoon. Mix in the confectioners' sugar with enough soy cream to make a filling with a thick, spreadable consistency.

3 Add a little filling to the brownie crumbs and use your hands to mix it in. Gradually add more filling and use your hands to knead the mixture together. Continue to add filling until the mixture can be squeezed into small balls that hold together. Cover the bowl with plastic wrap and refrigerate the mixture for 30 minutes.

4 Line a baking sheet with parchment paper. Roll the cake mixture into 24 small balls and place them on the prepared sheet. Push a lollipop stick into each ball. Put the cake pops on the sheet into the freezer for 30 minutes until firm.

5 Melt the chocolate in the microwave, using short 30-second bursts, or in a double boiler or a heatproof bowl set over a saucepan of gently simmering water. Put the coconut into a shallow bowl. Dip each cake pop into the melted chocolate, then into the coconut, turning so that each cake pop is well covered. Place in a holder or on the lined baking sheet to cool. Let sit until the chocolate is firm before serving.

1 chocolate brownie cake (see page 94), but made without macadamia nuts

24 lollipop sticks

6 ounces vegan and gluten-free semisweet chocolate, broken into pieces

¾ cup dry unsweetened coconut

ICING

2 tablespoons packed vegan and gluten-free margarine

2 tablespoons packed vegetable shortening

1¾ cups vegan and gluten-free confectioners' sugar

¼ cup gluten-free soy cream

Cook's tip

If you use your hands to mix the cake crumbs and the filling, instead of a spoon or mixer, it will be easier to tell when you have the right consistency to make the cake pops.

Cook's tip

You might be tempted to add a tiny drop of green food coloring to the peppermint cream filling, but remember it's best to keep the color subtle instead of garishly green.

Chocolate & Peppermint
WHOOPIE PIES

These little treats will have you wanting seconds—you might find yourself making another batch sooner than you think!

1 Preheat the oven to 400°F. Line two large baking sheets with parchment paper. Make up the egg replacer in a small bowl according to the package directions, and beat it with a fork for a minute, until bubbly.

2 Cream together the margarine, sugar, egg replacer, and glycerin in a large bowl. Sift the remaining dry ingredients into the mixture, add the soy milk, and quickly stir it all together.

3 Use two teaspoons to shape 20 small regular balls of the batter and place them on the prepared baking sheets. Bake in the preheated oven for 10 minutes, or until puffy and cooked through. Test with your finger—they should be soft but not sticky. Transfer to wire racks to cool.

4 To make the peppermint cream filling, beat together the margarine, vegetable shortening, confectioners' sugar, soy cream, and peppermint extract with a fork until smooth. Spread or pipe the filling onto the flat side of half of the cake bottoms, then sandwich together with the remaining cakes and serve.

vegan and gluten-free egg replacer, equivalent to 2 eggs

½ cup firmly packed vegan and gluten-free margarine

½ cup vegan superfine or granulated sugar

1 teaspoon vegan glycerin

1 cup gluten-free all-purpose flour

1 teaspoon gluten-free baking powder

½ teaspoon gluten-free baking soda

¼ teaspoon xanthan gum

⅓ cup vegan and gluten-free unsweetened cocoa powder

⅓ cup gluten-free soy milk

FILLING

3 tablespoons packed vegan and gluten-free margarine

3 tablespoons packed vegetable shortening

1¼ cups vegan and gluten-free confectioners' sugar

2 tablespoons gluten-free soy cream

½ teaspoon peppermint extract

Orange & Cinnamon MUFFINS

A surprise marmalade center makes these sugar-topped cinnamon muffins a delicious treat for breakfast time.

1 Preheat the oven to 350°F. Line a 12-section muffin pan with paper cups.

2 Sift the flour, baking powder, and xanthan gum into a large mixing bowl. Stir in the ground almonds, cinnamon, orange zest, and sugar and mix well with a wooden spoon.

3 Mix the oil, yogurt, and milk together in a small bowl. Pour the wet mixture over the dry ingredients and stir with a wooden spatula until just combined.

4 Put 2 teaspoons of the batter into the bottom of each paper cup and use the back of the spoon to spread out the batter, if necessary, so that the bottoms are completely covered. Put a teaspoon of marmalade into each muffin cup. Divide the remaining muffin batter equally among the muffin cups. Sprinkle each muffin with brown sugar and cinnamon.

5 Bake in the preheated oven for 20–25 minutes, or until the muffins are golden. Press the surface of one of the muffins with the back of a teaspoon to check whether it springs back. Transfer the muffins to a wire rack to cool (and to let the sugar topping become crisp) before serving.

1⅓ cups gluten-free all-purpose flour

1½ teaspoons gluten-free baking powder

½ teaspoon xanthan gum

⅓ cup ground almonds

2 teaspoons ground cinnamon

zest of 1 unwaxed orange

¾ cup vegan granulated sugar

⅓ cup canola oil

¼ cup gluten-free soy yogurt

1 cup gluten-free soy milk

¼ cup gluten-free, unwaxed orange marmalade

TOPPING

¼ cup firmly packed vegan light brown sugar

1 tablespoon ground cinnamon

Cook's tip

A sweet, fruity marmalade works well here, but you could experiment with a tangy unwaxed Seville orange preserves or make a variation with unwaxed lemon marmalade.

Cook's tip

It is best to bake these muffins in the center of the oven and not on the top shelf. This is so that the topping doesn't brown too quickly before the muffins are cooked in the center.

Carrot & Pecan MUFFINS

*These muffins are classic favorites and are enhanced by the
added crunchy, spiced topping.*

1 Preheat the oven to 350°F. Line a 12-section muffin pan with paper cups.

2 To make the topping, put the finely chopped pecans into a small bowl. Stir in the sugar and allspice. Set aside.

3 Beat the sugar and oil together in a large mixing bowl, then stir in the flour, baking powder, xanthan gum, and allspice and mix thoroughly. Add the carrots and coarsely chopped pecans and stir with a wooden spoon until the batter is well combined.

4 Divide the batter equally among the muffin cups. Sprinkle the topping mixture over the muffins.

5 Bake in the preheated oven for 25–30 minutes, or until a toothpick inserted into the center of a muffin comes out clean. Transfer to a wire rack to cool.

1 cup firmly packed vegan brown sugar

¾ cup canola oil

1¾ cups gluten-free all-purpose flour

2¼ teaspoons gluten-free baking powder

½ teaspoon xanthan gum

½ teaspoon ground allspice

3 cups shredded carrots

2 cups coarsely chopped pecans

TOPPING

¾ cup finely chopped pecans

3 tablespoons packed vegan brown sugar

½ teaspoon ground allspice

Mango & Coconut MUFFINS

These muffins have a taste of the Caribbean, with fresh, ripe mango and coconut flavors.

1 Preheat the oven to 375°F. Line a muffin pan with ten paper cups.

2 Sift together the flour and baking powder into a large bowl. Mix in the flaxseed meal, coconut, and sugar.

3 Crush the cardamom pods and remove the seeds. Discard the green pods. Crush the seeds finely in a mortar and pestle or with a rolling pin and stir into the mixture.

4 Whisk together the soy milk and oil in a small bowl and stir into the mixture, adding the mango at the same time. Mix until just combined; do not overmix.

5 Divide the batter among the ten cups in the prepared muffin pan and sprinkle the top of each muffin with a little of the extra coconut. Bake in the preheated oven for 25–30 minutes, or until a toothpick inserted into the center of a muffin comes out clean. Let cool for 5 minutes before removing from the pan.

2 cups gluten-free all-purpose flour

1 tablespoon gluten-free baking powder

1 tablespoon flaxseed meal

¾ cup dry unsweetened coconut, plus 2 tablespoons for topping

½ cup vegan superfine or granulated sugar

9 cardamom pods

¾ cup gluten-free soy milk

⅓ cup canola oil

1 large fresh, ripe unwaxed mango, peeled, pitted, and chopped

Cook's tip

For an alternative flavor, you could replace the mango with chopped unwaxed guava, if you prefer.

Coffee & Walnut MUFFINS

These deliciously nutty muffins are a great choice for a breakfast on the go!

1 Preheat the oven to 350°F. Line a 12-section muffin pan with paper cups.

2 Sift together the flour, baking powder, espresso powder, and cinnamon into a large bowl and stir in the superfine sugar.

3 Whisk together the soy milk, oil, and vanilla extract in a small bowl. Stir into the dry ingredients, adding the chopped walnuts at the same time. Mix until just combined; do not overmix.

4 Divide the batter equally among the paper cups in the prepared muffin pan and sprinkle the top of each muffin with the finely chopped walnuts and brown sugar. Bake in the preheated oven for 20–25 minutes, or until a toothpick inserted into a muffin comes out clean. Let cool slightly for 5 minutes before removing from the pan and serving.

2¼ cups gluten-free all-purpose flour

1 tablespoon gluten-free baking powder

2 tablespoons gluten-free espresso powder

1 teaspoon ground cinnamon

1 cup vegan superfine or granulated sugar

1 cup gluten-free soy milk

⅓ cup canola oil

1 tablespoon vanilla extract

1 cup chopped walnuts

TOPPING

¼ cup finely chopped walnuts

1 tablespoon packed vegan light brown sugar

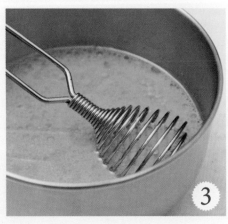

Peach & Vanilla MUFFINS

Opinions are divided over whether muffins should ever be frosted,
but the sticky peach glaze used here makes a delicious alternative.

3–4 ripe unwaxed peaches
   (about 1 pound), pitted

juice of ½ unwaxed lemon

3 tablespoons maple syrup

2¾ cups gluten-free all-purpose flour

1 teaspoon gluten-free baking powder

½ teaspoon gluten-free baking soda

1 teaspoon flaxseed meal

½ cup firmly packed vegan light brown
   sugar

½ cup gluten-free soy milk

1 tablespoon vegan and gluten-free
   white wine vinegar

1 tablespoon vanilla extract

⅓ cup canola oil

¼ cup gluten-free, unwaxed
   peach preserves

1 Preheat the oven to 350°F. Line a 12-section muffin pan with paper cups.

2 Cut the peaches into eighths. Place in a shallow baking dish. Pour the lemon juice and maple syrup over the peaches and bake in the preheated oven for 15 minutes. Set aside to cool completely and leave the oven on.

3 Sift the flour, baking powder, and baking soda into a large mixing bowl. Stir in the flaxseed meal and sugar. Put the soy milk into a small bowl, stir in the vinegar, and set aside for a few minutes to curdle.

4 Put half of the baked peaches and the juice from the baking dish into the bowl of a food processor. Add the vanilla extract and canola oil and pulse the mixture to a puree. Coarsely chop the remaining baked peaches.

5 Stir the milk mixture and peach puree into the dry ingredients, using a rubber spatula, until just combined. Fold in the chopped peaches.

6 Divide the batter equally among the paper cups and bake in the preheated oven for 20–25 minutes, or until risen and springy to the touch. Transfer to a wire rack to cool.

7 To make the peach icing, put the peach preserves into a small saucepan with 1 tablespoon of water. Bring to a boil, stirring continuously with a wooden spoon, and boil vigorously for 1 minute. Remove the pan from the heat and continue to stir for an additional 30 seconds. Brush the warm glaze over the muffins and let cool before serving.

White Chocolate BROWNIES

These chewy treats are also surprisingly packed with protein, thanks to the tofu in this recipe.

1 Preheat the oven to 325°F. Line a 9-inch square baking pan with parchment paper so that the paper extends beyond the edge of the pan.

2 Put the tofu, milk, and oil into the bowl of a food processor and process until smooth. Pour the mixture into a large mixing bowl and use a spatula to scrape the sides of the bowl.

3 Add the brown sugar, superfine sugar, and vanilla and beat together with a wooden spoon. Stir in the flour, xanthan gum, baking powder, baking soda, and salt and mix well. Fold the chocolate into the batter.

4 Spoon the batter into the prepared pan and use a spatula to push it into the corners and smooth the top. Bake in the center of the preheated oven for 30 minutes, then remove from the oven—the texture will become firm as the brownies cool. Let cool in the pan for 10 minutes, then lift the parchment paper and transfer the brownie, still on the paper, to a wire rack and let cool completely before slicing.

3 ounces extra firm silken tofu

¼ cup gluten-free soy milk

¼ cup canola oil

½ cup firmly packed vegan light brown sugar

½ cup vegan superfine or granulated sugar

1 teaspoon vanilla extract

1¾ cups gluten-free all-purpose flour

½ teaspoon xanthan gum

½ teaspoon gluten-free baking powder

½ teaspoon gluten-free baking soda

¼ teaspoon salt

4 ounces vegan and gluten-free white chocolate, chopped into small pieces

Cook's tip

Brands of vegan white chocolate vary; some will melt, while others bake to a toffeelike consistency—both of which can be good in brownies.

Chocolate & Macadamia
BROWNIES

These rich and chocolaty brownies are a wonderful midmorning treat with a cup of tea or coffee.

1 Preheat the oven to 350°F. Grease and line an 8-inch square baking pan with parchment paper so that the paper extends beyond the edge of the pan.

2 Mix the flaxseed meal with 3 tablespoons of water and set aside for 10 minutes.

3 Sift together the flour, xanthan gum, baking soda, and cocoa powder in a large bowl. Add the sugar and combine thoroughly.

4 Break the chocolate into small pieces, put into a small heatproof bowl, and pour ¼ cup of boiling water over it. Stir thoroughly to melt the chocolate.

5 Stir the flaxseed paste, melted chocolate, vanilla extract, glycerin, melted margarine, and chopped nuts into the dry ingredients. Use your hands to form the mixture into a soft dough. Press the dough into the prepared baking pan.

6 Bake in the preheated oven for 30 minutes, or until crisp around the edges but the center is still soft. Carefully lift the brownie out of the pan, using the lining paper. Leaving on the paper, place on a wire rack to cool for 10 minutes. Carefully peel away the paper and cut into nine squares. Let cool completely before serving.

2 tablespoons flaxseed meal

1¾ cups gluten-free all-purpose flour

1 teaspoon xanthan gum

¼ teaspoon gluten-free baking soda

⅔ cup vegan and gluten-free unsweetened cocoa powder

1¼ cups firmly packed vegan light brown sugar

1 ounce vegan and gluten-free semisweet chocolate

2 teaspoons vanilla extract

½ teaspoon vegan glycerin

⅓ cup firmly packed vegan and gluten-free margarine, melted, plus extra for greasing

⅓ cup coarsely chopped macadamia nuts

CHAPTER 3
Cookies & Bars

Chocolate COOKIES

These are pretty enough to give away to friends as gifts, and they are also fun for children to make.

vegan and gluten-free egg replacer, equivalent to 1 egg

⅔ cup gluten-free all-purpose flour

¼ cup vegan and gluten-free unsweetened cocoa powder

½ teaspoon gluten-free baking powder

2 tablespoons packed vegan and gluten-free margarine

½ cup vegan superfine or granulated sugar

⅓ cup vegan and gluten-free confectioners' sugar

1 Make up the egg replacer in a small bowl according to the package directions, and beat it with a fork for a minute, until bubbly.

2 Sift the flour, cocoa, and baking powder into a large mixing bowl (this is important to make sure the cookies are evenly colored without any white flecks). Add the margarine and use your fingers to rub it in. When the mixture has a light, crumbly texture, add the superfine sugar and egg replacer, then beat together using an electric mixer. If you don't have an electric mixer, you can do this by hand with a wooden spoon, but it may take several minutes for the mixture to come together to form a dough. When the dough is clumping together, gather it into a ball, wrap it in plastic wrap, and place in the refrigerator to chill for 30 minutes.

3 Preheat the oven to 350°F. Line a large baking sheet with parchment paper.

4 Put the confectioners' sugar onto a plate and spread it out. Use a sharp knife to divide the dough into 12 equal pieces. Roll each piece into a small ball, and then gently roll the ball in the confectioners' sugar until it is completely coated. Place the cookies on the prepared baking sheet, leaving a little space around each so that they can spread. Bake in the preheated oven for 10–12 minutes, then transfer the cookies to a wire rack until completely cool before serving.

Cook's tip

If you're cooking for adults, you could customize these treats by adding a splash of vegan amaretto or hazelnut liqueur to the mixture at the same time as the egg replacer.

3

4

5

Ice Cream SANDWICH COOKIES

These are a great treat when served straight from the freezer on a hot afternoon.

1 Preheat the oven to 300°F and cover a large baking sheet with parchment paper.

2 Put the rice flour, cocoa powder, baking powder, and salt into a large mixing bowl and mix well with a wooden spoon.

3 Place the dates in the bowl of a food processor with the vanilla extract, nut butter, and 3 tablespoons of milk. Process to a creamy paste.

4 Stir the date paste into the flour mixture and gradually add up to another 2–3 tablespoons of milk. Use your hands to bring the mixture together to form a dough that is soft but not sticky.

5 Turn out the dough onto a lightly floured board and roll it to about ⅛ inch thick. Use a 2½-inch cookie cutter to cut out 24 cookies, rerolling the dough scraps as necessary.

6 Place the cookies on the prepared baking sheet. Bake in the preheated oven for 15–20 minutes, or until changing color at the edges. Let cool a little on the baking sheet, then transfer the cookies to a wire rack to cool completely.

7 When the cookies are completely cool, take your ice cream out of the freezer and let it defrost until just spoonable but not runny. Quickly sandwich two of the cookies together with 2–3 teaspoons of ice cream, then repeat to create 12 sandwiches in total. Return any unused ice cream to the freezer. Arrange the cookies on a baking sheet and freeze for at least an hour. Serve straight from the freezer.

1 cup rice flour, plus extra
  for dusting

½ cup vegan and gluten-free
  cocoa powder

½ teaspoon gluten-free baking powder

pinch of salt

1½ cups chopped pitted, unwaxed dates

1 teaspoon vanilla extract

2 tablespoons nut butter

about ⅓ cup almond or hazelnut milk

½–¾ cup vegan and gluten-free
  ice cream, to serve

Cook's tip

Almond or hazelnut milk
or butter both work well
in this recipe.

Lime ICED COOKIES

Everybody loves an iced cookie. These are best eaten on the day they are made, but they are so delicious they probably won't last for a day.

1 Make up the egg replacer in a small bowl according to the package directions, and beat it with a fork for a minute, until bubbly.

2 Put the flour, baking powder, and salt into a large mixing bowl. Add the margarine and rub it in with your fingers. Stir in the sugar. Add the lime zest, glycerin, and egg replacer. Use your hands to work the mixture into a ball and transfer it to a lightly floured board. Knead the dough and shape it into a log that is about 6 inches long. Wrap it tightly in plastic wrap and chill in the refrigerator for 1 hour.

3 Preheat the oven to 400°F and line a large baking sheet with parchment paper.

4 Take the cookie dough out of the refrigerator, unwrap it, and place on a lightly floured board. Using a serrated knife and a gentle sawing motion, slice the log into 12 cookies. Transfer the cookies to the prepared baking sheet.

5 Bake in the preheated oven for 15 minutes, or until just browning at the edges. Be careful—they may brown underneath more quickly than they do on top. Take the cookies out of the oven and transfer immediately to a wire rack to cool completely.

6 Put the confectioners' sugar, 5 teaspoons of the lime juice, and the corn syrup in a small saucepan over low heat, and heat, stirring continously, until thickened to a pouring consistency but not too thin. Spread a little fondant icing onto each cookie, decorate with a few pieces of lime zest strips, and set aside to let the icing to set before serving.

vegan and gluten-free egg replacer, equivalent to 1 egg

1⅔ cups gluten-free all-purpose flour, plus extra for dusting

½ teaspoon gluten-free baking powder

pinch of salt

⅓ cup firmly packed vegan and gluten-free margarine

⅓ cup vegan superfine or granulated sugar

juice and zest of 1 unwaxed lime

1 teaspoon vegan glycerin

1¼ cups vegan and gluten-free confectioners' sugar

2 teaspoons light corn syrup

strips of unwaxed lime zest, to decorate

Cook's tip

A zesting tool will enable you to create long strips of zest for decorating cakes. The fondant icing dries to a shiny finish, which looks great on cookies. For a simple icing, mix ½ cup confectioners' sugar with a little lime juice.

Cook's tip

These cookies (without their filling) can be used in recipes that require gluten-free cookie crumbs to make cookie crusts, such as the Ice Cream Pie (page 148) in this book.

Peanut Butter SANDWICH COOKIES

These easy sandwich cookies are packed with protein from gluten-free oats and peanut butter—making them a great reward with a glass of chilled soy milk after an exercise session.

1 Preheat the oven to 350°F. Line a large baking sheet with parchment paper.

2 Make up the egg replacer in a small bowl according to the package directions, and beat it with a fork for a minute, until bubbly.

3 Sift the flour and baking powder into a large mixing bowl. Add the oats, sugar, margarine, egg replacer, and peanut butter. Using an electric mixer, beat together on a slow speed for 2 minutes, or until the mixture comes together in clumps. Alternatively, place the ingredients in a large mixing bowl and beat with a fork.

4 Turn the dough onto a floured board and pat it into a cylinder shape. Use a sharp knife to divide it into 12 equal pieces, then cut each piece in half again to form 24 pieces. Roll each piece of dough into a ball and place on the prepared baking sheet. Flatten each ball so that they are no more than ½ inch thick.

5 Bake in the preheated oven for 15 minutes, or until just golden. Lift the parchment paper to transfer the cookies to a wire rack and let cool for 15 minutes, until firm, before removing from the paper. Let cool completely before adding the filling.

6 To make the filling, beat together the peanut butter, confectioners' sugar, cocoa, and margarine until they are thoroughly combined and the mixture is smooth. The easiest way to do this is to put all the ingredients in a large mixing bowl and use an electric mixer, but you can also do it with a fork.

7 When the cookies are cool, spread half of them generously with the chocolate peanut butter filling and sandwich together with the remaining cookies.

vegan and gluten-free egg replacer, equivalent to 1 egg

1¼ cups gluten-free all-purpose flour, plus extra for dusting

1 teaspoon gluten-free baking powder

1¼ cups gluten-free oats

½ cup firmly packed vegan light brown sugar

½ cup firmly packed vegan and gluten-free margarine

⅓ cup chunky peanut butter

FILLING

⅔ cup chunky peanut butter

⅓ cup vegan and gluten-free confectioners' sugar

½ cup vegan and gluten-free unsweetened cocoa powder

¼ cup firmly packed vegan and gluten-free margarine

Mocha COOKIES

These cookies have strong coffee and chocolate flavors and are great when accompanied by a vegan milky coffee or hot chocolate.

1 Preheat the oven to 350°F. Line a large baking sheet with parchment paper.

2 Sift together the flour, baking powder, and cocoa powder in a large mixing bowl. Add the sugar and combine thoroughly.

3 Dissolve the espresso powder in 1 tablespoon of boiling water and stir into the bowl. Add the margarine and oats and mix thoroughly to form a soft dough.

4 Form the dough into 14 small balls, place on the prepared baking sheet, and flatten slightly. Leave spaces between the cookies because they will expand during cooking. Bake in the preheated oven for 15 minutes, or until crisp. Transfer to a wire rack to cool, using a spatula. Let cool completely before serving or storing in an airtight jar for up to five days.

1 cup gluten-free all-purpose flour

¼ teaspoon gluten-free baking powder

3 tablespoons vegan and gluten-free unsweetened cocoa powder

½ cup firmly packed vegan brown sugar

1 tablespoon gluten-free espresso powder

½ cup firmly packed vegan and gluten-free margarine

½ cup gluten-free rolled oats

Black Pepper
SHORTBREAD

These crumbly shortbread cookies have a warm peppery taste and are a perfect treat for a chilly day.

1 Preheat the oven to 375°F and line a 10- x 7-inch baking pan with parchment paper.

2 Put all the ingredients into a large mixing bowl and, using an electric mixer, mix on a slow speed until the ingredients are thoroughly combined. The mixture will develop a bread crumblike consistency after a minute and will start to clump together a few seconds later. Alternatively, put the sugar and margarine into a large mixing bowl and cream together with a fork until thoroughly combined. Add the rice flour, cornstarch, and black pepper, and mix with a wooden spoon until all the ingredients are thoroughly combined. The mixture will have a bread crumb-like texture but should hold together when you pinch a little between your thumb and index finger.

3 Transfer the dough to the lined pan and press into an even layer. Use a sharp knife to mark the surface of the dough into 12 equal pieces. You can also use a fork to prick decorative patterns on the cookies.

4 Bake in the preheated oven for 15 minutes, or until lightly golden. While the dough is still warm in the baking pan, cut it into pieces along the lines you made before baking. Let firm in the pan before gently transferring to a wire rack to cool completely.

¾ cup rice flour

¾ cup gluten-free cornstarch

⅓ cup vegan superfine or granulated sugar

½ cup firmly packed vegan and gluten-free margarine

½ teaspoon ground black pepper

Cook's tip

Try using cinnamon in place of black pepper and serve with warm, baked unwaxed apples.

③

④

④

Salted Almond BISCOTTI

Chunky toasted almonds give these crunchy cookies their traditional texture, and a little sea salt adds a contemporary twist.

1 Preheat the oven to 350°F.

2 Put the almonds onto a large baking sheet and bake them in the preheated oven for 8 minutes, or until fragrant. Set aside to cool, then coarsely chop them. Line the baking sheet with parchment paper. Make up the egg replacer in a small bowl according to the package directions, and beat it with a fork for a minute, until bubbly.

3 Put the flour, sugar, baking powder, and xanthan gum into a large mixing bowl and mix thoroughly with a wooden spoon. Stir in the egg replacer, almonds, salt, and vanilla. Use your hands to knead the mixture together to form a dough. Don't be tempted to add any water—it will come together.

4 Turn out the dough onto a floured board and cut into two pieces. Shape each piece into a flattened log around 12 inches long. Transfer to the baking sheet and bake for 30–35 minutes, or until beginning to brown. Remove from the oven and carefully transfer to a cutting board. Using an oven mitt to hold the hot dough, carefully slice each log diagonally into ten slices. Lay the slices flat on the baking sheet and return to the oven for an additional 10 minutes. Transfer to a wire rack to cool.

5 Break the chocolate into small pieces and melt in a microwave, using short 30-second bursts, or in a double boiler or heatproof bowl set over a saucepan of gently simmering water. Dip each biscotti into the melted chocolate and use a pastry brush to make sure each one is coated halfway. Place on a sheet of parchment paper to dry.

1 cup whole almonds with skins

vegan and gluten-free egg replacer, equivalent to 4 eggs

2⅓ cups gluten-free all-purpose flour, plus extra for dusting

1 cup vegan superfine or granulated sugar

½ teaspoon gluten-free baking powder

1 teaspoon xanthan gum

½ teaspoon coarsely ground sea salt

1 teaspoon vanilla extract

6 ounces vegan and gluten-free semisweet chocolate, to decorate

Cook's tip
If you're cutting down on salt, replace it in this recipe with a tablespoon of unwaxed lemon or orange zest.

Earl Grey COOKIES

*Serve these crisp cookies as an accompaniment to a fruit salad or
compote—or with a cup of hot tea!*

2 tablespoons Earl Grey tea leaves

1½ cups gluten-free all-purpose flour,
    plus extra for dusting

⅔ cup rice flour

½ teaspoon salt

vegan and gluten-free egg replacer,
    equivalent to 1 egg

¾ cup plus 2 tablespoons firmly packed
    vegan and gluten-free margarine

¾ cup vegan and gluten-free
    confectioners' sugar

zest of 1 unwaxed lemon

½ cup vegan superfine or granulated
    sugar

1 Chop the tea leaves finely. If you have an electric coffee grinder or spice
grinder, process the tea leaves to a fine powder. Put the tea into a large
mixing bowl and stir in the flours and salt. Make up the egg replacer in a
small bowl according to the package directions, and beat it with a fork for a
minute, until bubbly.

2 Beat the margarine and confectioners' sugar together until creamy.
You can use an electric mixer or do it by hand with a wooden spoon.
Gradually incorporate the egg replacer and lemon zest. Stir in the flours,
tea, and salt and mix to a dough.

3 Turn out the dough onto a lightly floured board and gather it into a ball
with your hands. Shape the dough into a log that is about 12 inches long
and pat it into shape so that slices will be rectangular. Wrap it tightly in plastic
wrap and refrigerate for 1 hour.

4 Preheat the oven to 350°F and cover a large baking sheet with parchment
paper. Put the superfine sugar into a small bowl.

5 Take the cookie dough out of the refrigerator, unwrap it, and place it on
a cutting board. Using a sharp serrated knife and a gentle sawing motion,
cut the log into two equal pieces, then cut each piece into 16 slices. Dip each
slice into the bowl of sugar, coating only one side. Place the cookies, sugar
side up, on the prepared baking sheet.

6 Bake in the preheated oven for 20–25 minutes, or until just golden. Let
the cookies cool on the baking sheet for a few minutes, then use a spatula
to transfer them to a wire rack to cool completely.

Cook's tip

It's important to turn the sheets during cooking so that the thin edges of the cookies do not burn.

Hazelnut THINS

With crispy, wavy edges and soft, chewy centers, these nutty cookies are everybody's favorites.

1 Make up the egg replacer in a small bowl according to the package directions, and beat it with a fork for a minute, until bubbly.

2 Put the flour, ground hazelnuts, baking soda, and salt into a large mixing bowl and stir together with a wooden spoon. In a separate bowl, cream the margarine and sugars together with an electric mixer or wooden spoon, then beat in the egg replacer and vanilla. Spoon the wet mixture into the dry mixture and mix thoroughly. Use your hands to bring the dough into a ball, wrap in plastic wrap, and chill in the refrigerator for 1 hour.

3 Preheat the oven to 350°F and line two large baking sheets with parchment paper.

4 Take the cookie dough out of the refrigerator, unwrap it, and place on a lightly floured board. Roll into 24 small balls and place them on the prepared baking sheets, leaving plenty of room for the cookies to spread as they bake.

5 Bake in the preheated oven for 15 minutes, rotating the sheets after 10 minutes. Let the cookies cool for 5 minutes, until firm, before lifting the parchment paper onto wire racks. Let the cookies cool completely before taking them off the paper.

vegan and gluten-free egg replacer, equivalent to 2 eggs

2⅔ cups gluten-free all-purpose flour, plus extra for dusting

½ cup ground hazelnuts

1 teaspoon gluten-free baking soda

1 teaspoon sea salt

1 cup firmly packed vegan and gluten-free margarine

1 cup vegan superfine or granulated sugar

¾ cup firmly packed vegan brown sugar

1 teaspoon vanilla extract

Caramel Peach BARS

Juicy peach slices covered with sticky caramel sauce and a crunchy crumb layer. These slices will be a popular contribution to a bake sale!

1 Preheat the oven to 350°F. Grease a 10 x 15-inch baking pan and line with parchment paper.

2 To make the bottom layer, put the margarine and sugar into a large mixing bowl and cream them together using a fork. Stir in the flour, oats, and baking powder and knead together with your hands until it forms a sticky dough. Set aside one-third of the dough to use in the topping. Transfer the rest of the dough to the prepared baking pan and press it into a smooth layer covering the bottom of the pan. Bake in the preheated oven for 20 minutes, then remove from the oven and set aside to cool. Leave the oven on.

3 To make the topping, put the reserved dough into a large mixing bowl and add the gluten-free oats. Use the tips of your fingers to rub the oats into the mixture. Sprinkle the mixture onto another baking pan and bake for 20 minutes, or until crisp and golden, then let cool.

4 Drain the peach slices, then arrange them in overlapping rows over the cooled bottom layer.

5 To make the caramel topping, put the sugar, margarine, and soy cream into a saucepan and heat gently, stirring constantly, to melt the ingredients together. Cook over low heat for 5 minutes, or until the sugar has completely dissolved. Remove from the heat and stir in the vanilla. Spoon the warm caramel over the peaches. Avoid putting caramel at the edges of the baking pan, because this can make it difficult to get the bars out of the pan. Sprinkle the crispy crumb topping over the caramel and set aside for about 30 minutes, until the caramel has cooled completely.

6 Carefully lift the cooled mixture out of the baking pan, keeping the parchment paper underneath it to support it, and place on a cutting board. Use a sharp knife to cut into 18 bars.

BOTTOM LAYER

1 cup firmly packed vegan and gluten-free margarine, plus extra for greasing

1 cup firmly packed vegan brown sugar

2⅓ cups gluten-free all-purpose flour

2¼ cups gluten-free rolled oats

1 teaspoon gluten-free baking powder

TOPPING

½ cup gluten-free rolled oats

2 (15-ounce) cans unwaxed peach slices

⅔ cup firmly packed vegan brown sugar

¼ cup firmly packed vegan and gluten-free margarine

3 tablespoons gluten-free soy cream

½ teaspoon vanilla extract

Cook's tip

Canned peach slices make an elegant and professional-looking topping for these bars, but you can use fresh peaches instead—you'll need around eight unwaxed peaches.

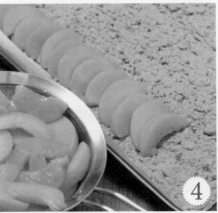

Coconut SQUARES

Traditionally, coconut squares are made with condensed milk, but coconut cream makes a tasty alternative.

1 Line a 7-inch square baking pan with plastic wrap.

2 Put the coconut cream into a large saucepan with the sugar. Heat gently to melt the coconut cream and the sugar. Bring to boiling point and then simmer, stirring continuously, for 20 minutes to reduce the mixture to a thick syrup. If you have a candy thermometer, check that the temperature is around jam-setting point (220°F). If you don't have a candy thermometer, drop a little of the syrup onto a cold plate, wait for a minute, and then carefully test it with your finger. It's ready when the surface wrinkles when you push the edge.

3 Stir in the coconut and cardamom powder, mix thoroughly with a wooden spoon, and then spoon half of the dough into the lined baking pan. Press down firmly to form a smooth layer in the bottom of the pan. Mix the beet powder with 2 teaspoons of water and then mix it into the remaining coconut mixture. Make sure it is well distributed. Spoon the pink coconut into the pan and press it into a firm layer on top of the white coconut.

4 Put the coconut mixture into a refrigerator to chill for at least 4 hours, or overnight. Then turn it out of the pan and use a sharp knife to cut it into 20 squares.

1 cup coconut cream

1¼ cups vegan superfine or granulated sugar

4¼ cups dry unsweetened coconut

1 teaspoon ground cardamom

¼ teaspoon beet powder

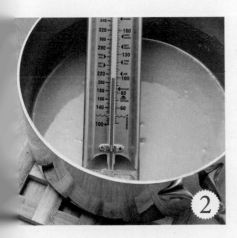

Lemon RIPPLE BARS

These soft lemony bars are a wonderful afternoon treat. Cut them into smaller squares for a sophisticated get-together.

BOTTOM LAYER

¾ cup gluten-free cornstarch

¾ cup rice flour

⅓ cup vegan superfine or granulated sugar

½ cup firmly packed vegan and gluten-free margarine

FILLING

vegan and gluten-free egg replacer, equivalent to 3 eggs

½ cup firmly packed vegan and gluten-free margarine

½ cup vegan superfine or granulated sugar

1 teaspoon vanilla extract

2 tablespoons gluten-free all-purpose flour

¾ cup ground almonds

LEMON CURD

1 teaspoon gluten-free cornstarch

juice of ½ unwaxed lemon

2½ tablespoons packed vegan and gluten-free margarine

3 tablespoons vegan superfine or granulated sugar

1 Preheat the oven to 350°F and line a 10 x 7-inch baking pan with parchment paper.

2 Place all the bottom layer ingredients into a mixing bowl and, using an electric mixer, mix on a slow speed until the ingredients are thoroughly combined. The dough will develop a bread crumblike consistency after a minute and will start to clump together a few seconds later. Alternatively, place the margarine and sugar in a large mixing bowl and cream together with a fork until thoroughly combined. Add the rice flour and cornstarch and mix with a wooden spoon until all the ingredients are thoroughly combined. The dough will have a breadcrumb-like texture but should hold together when you pinch a little between your thumb and index finger. Transfer the dough to the prepared pan and press into an even layer.

3 To make the filling, make up the egg replacer in a small bowl according to the package directions, and beat it with a fork for a minute, until bubbly. Cream together the margarine, sugar, egg replacer, and vanilla extract with a wooden spoon in a large mixing bowl. Mix in the flour and ground almonds. Spoon the filling over the bottom layer and smooth the top with a spatula.

4 To make the lemon curd, put the cornstarch into a small bowl and mix it to a paste with a little lemon juice. Put the rest of the lemon juice into a saucepan with the margarine and sugar, and heat gently, stirring, until the margarine has melted and the sugar has dissolved. Add the cornstarch mixture and continue to cook for an additional 2–3 minutes, or until the mixture has thickened but is still pourable. Drizzle about ½ cup of lemon curd over the filling. Use a knife to drag the lemon curd through the almond filling but don't overmix.

5 Bake in the preheated oven for 25 minutes, or until the almond filling is puffy and golden—the lemon curd will still be wet but will become firm as it cools. Let cool in the pan, then carefully lift out, using the paper to support it, and cut into bars with a sharp knife.

Cook's tip

Line the bottom and sides of the pan with a single piece of parchment paper and let the paper overhang the pan to make the bars easy to lift out after baking.

Rocky Road SLICES

*A firm favorite with children and adults alike. Small portions are best
for this sweet treat.*

1 Preheat the oven to 350°F. Grease an 8 x 12-inch baking pan and line with parchment paper.

2 To make the bottom layer, put the margarine and sugar into a large mixing bowl and cream them together using a fork. Stir in the flour, xanthan gum, and cocoa and mix with a wooden spoon until the cocoa is well dispersed. Transfer to the prepared baking pan and use the tips of your fingers to press into a smooth layer covering the bottom of the pan. Bake in the preheated oven for 15–20 minutes, then set aside to cool.

3 To make the topping, put the chocolate into a double boiler or a heatproof bowl set over a saucepan of simmering water. Add the margarine and light corn syrup and melt the ingredients, stirring with a metal spoon, until smooth. Set aside to cool a little.

4 If the marshmallows you are using are large, cut them into quarters, or use miniature marshmallows. Set half the marshmallows aside and stir the rest into the chocolate mixture along with the walnuts.

5 Pour the chocolate topping over the cooled bottom layer, spread it out with the back of a spoon, and sprinkle the reserved marshmallows over the top. Refrigerate for 2 hours until firm, then use a sharp knife to cut into bars.

BOTTOM LAYER

⅔ cup firmly packed vegan and gluten-free margarine, plus extra for greasing

⅓ cup vegan granulated sugar

1⅓ cups gluten-free all-purpose flour

1 teaspoon xanthan gum

¼ cup vegan and gluten-free unsweetened cocoa powder

TOPPING

12 ounces vegan and gluten-free semisweet chocolate, broken into pieces

1 cup firmly packed vegan and gluten-free margarine

1 tablespoon light corn syrup

4 ounces vegan marshmallows

¾ cup coarsely chopped walnuts

Cook's tip

Make sure you look for vegan marshmallows, because ordinary marshmallows are not suitable for vegans.

Pistachio COOKIES

These are dainty cookies that contain no flour and can be made in less than 25 minutes.

1 Preheat the oven to 350°F. Line a large baking sheet with parchment paper.

2 Put the pistachios into a heavy skillet and toast over low heat, stirring, until beginning to brown. Transfer to a plate and let cool completely.

3 Transfer the cooled pistachios to the bowl of a food processor fitted with a standard chopping blade. Add the maple syrup, sugar, and ginger and process until the mixture begins to clump together. If you don't have a food processor, chop the pistachios finely, put them into a large mixing bowl with the maple syrup, sugar, and ginger, and mix with a metal spoon until completely combined into a sticky dough.

4 Transfer the dough to a board, gently press into a thick log shape, and cut it into 16 equal pieces. Roll each piece into a ball, place on the prepared baking sheet, and flatten slightly. Bake in the preheated oven for 10–15 minutes, or until lightly browned. Lift the parchment paper onto a wire rack and let the cookies cool until firm.

5 Break the chocolate into small pieces and melt in a microwave in 30-second spurts, or in a double boiler or heatproof bowl set over a saucepan of simmering water. Drizzle the liquid chocolate over the cookies and let cool completely.

¾ cup shelled pistachio nuts

⅓ cup maple syrup

2 tablespoons packed vegan light brown sugar

1 teaspoon ground ginger

2 ounces vegan and gluten-free semisweet chocolate

Coffee & Date SLICES

Brandy and espresso with sweet dates make a tasty combination.
Omit the brandy if you're thinking of putting these into lunch bags.

1 Preheat the oven to 350°F and line an 8 x 10-inch baking pan with parchment paper.

2 Put the dates into a small saucepan with ⅓ cup of water and the brandy, if using. Cook over low heat for 2–3 minutes, or until the liquid has been absorbed, then remove from the heat.

3 Sift the flour and baking powder into a large mixing bowl. Stir in the almonds, flaxseed meal, and espresso powder and mix well with a wooden spoon.

4 Stir the dates, maple syrup, date syrup, and coconut oil into the dry ingredients and mix until thoroughly combined.

5 Transfer the dough to the prepared baking pan and use your fingers to press into a smooth layer. Sprinkle the brown sugar over the top.

6 Bake in the preheated oven for 15–20 minutes, then remove from the oven and mark into 12 equal slices. Let cool completely in the pan, then cut along the marks again and remove the slices piece by piece.

1⅓ cups pitted, unwaxed dates, finely chopped

2 tablespoons vegan brandy (optional)

⅔ cup gluten-free all-purpose flour

2½ teaspoons gluten-free baking powder

⅔ cup ground almonds

2 tablespoons flaxseed meal

2 tablespoons gluten-free espresso powder

2 tablespoons maple syrup

1 tablespoon unwaxed date syrup

2 tablespoons coconut oil

3 tablespoons packed vegan light brown sugar

Apricot & Raisin
OAT BARS

Perfect if you're counting calories, these fiber-rich cereal bars contain almost no fat but have plenty of flavor and are moist and chewy.

1 Put the apricots into a saucepan with enough water to cover. Heat over medium heat until almost boiling, then reduce the heat and simmer for 5 minutes, or until completely soft. Drain.

2 Put the apricots into a food processor with the sunflower oil and puree. Transfer the puree to a bowl and stir in the orange zest and the cardamom seeds, if using. Let cool.

3 Preheat the oven to 350°F. Brush an 8-inch square baking pan with oil.

4 Stir the raisins and oats into the apricot mixture. Spread out the dough in the prepared pan, leveling the surface with a spatula. Bake in the preheated oven for 35–40 minutes, or until firm. Cover with aluminum foil after about 25 minutes to prevent it from burning.

5 Let cool in the pan for 15 minutes. Turn out onto a wire rack and let cool completely before cutting into 12 bars.

2½ cups dried unwaxed apricots

2 tablespoons sunflower oil, plus extra for greasing

finely grated zest of ½ unwaxed orange

seeds from 5 cardamom pods, crushed (optional)

1 cup raisins

1¼ cups gluten-free rolled oats

Cook's tip
These cookies will keep for over a week in a sealed container, so it's worth making a double batch.

1

4

4

Peanut Butter
GRANOLA BARS

These chunky peanut butter bars are good for a breakfast on the go or lunch-bag snack.

1 Preheat the oven to 350°F. Grease a shallow 7 x 10-inch baking pan and line with parchment paper. Cut the paper a little larger than necessary so that the edges are above the edges of the baking pan; this will make it easier to lift the bars out.

2 Cream together the peanut butter, sugar, and light corn syrup. Using an electric mixer is the easiest way to do this, but you can use a wooden spoon. Stir in the granola and mix well. Put the dough into the prepared pan and use the back of a metal spoon to press it into a smooth layer.

3 Bake in the preheated oven for 25 minutes, or until golden brown. Carefully lift the baked granola bar out of the pan by holding the edges of the parchment paper. Let the parchment paper underneath for support and place on a wire rack to cool completely. When cool, use a sharp knife to cut into 12 bars.

vegan and gluten-free margarine, for greasing

⅓ cup chunky peanut butter

2 tablespoons packed vegan light brown sugar

2 tablespoons light corn syrup

3⅔ cups gluten-free granola

Maple & Pecan
GRANOLA BARS

The combination of maple and pecan is a classic flavor pairing and works really well in this tasty granola bar.

1 Preheat the oven to 350°F. Coat a 9 x 13-inch baking pan with vegetable oil spray.

2 Combine the oats, pecans, and almonds in a large baking pan and toast in the preheated oven for 5–7 minutes or until lightly browned.

3 Meanwhile, combine the maple syrup, brown sugar, and peanut butter in a small saucepan and bring to a boil over medium heat. Cook, stirring, for 4–5 minutes, or until the mixture thickens slightly. Stir in the vanilla extract and salt.

4 When the oats and nuts are toasted, put them into a mixing bowl and add the rice cereal and flaxseed meal. Add the syrup mixture to the oat mixture and stir to combine. Spread the syrup-oat mixture into the prepared baking pan and chill in the refrigerator for at least 1 hour before cutting into 12 bars. Serve at room temperature.

vegetable oil spray

2 cups gluten-free rolled oats

½ cup chopped pecans

½ cup slivered almonds

½ cup maple syrup

¼ cup firmly packed vegan light brown sugar

¼ cup creamy peanut butter

1 teaspoon vanilla extract

¼ teaspoon salt

2 cups gluten-free puffed rice cereal

¼ cup flaxseed meal

Cook's tip

If you prefer, you could swap the pecans for walnuts. You could also try adding some dried fruit.

CHAPTER 4

Desserts

Spiced Pumpkin PIE

A traditional-style pumpkin pie, flavored with warming spices and maple syrup.

FILLING

4 cups diced pumpkin flesh or
  1 (15-ounce) can 100 percent
  pure pumpkin puree (not pumpkin
  pie filling)

12 ounces firm silken tofu

½ cup maple syrup

1 teaspoon vanilla extract

½ teaspoon ground cinnamon

½ teaspoon ground nutmeg

½ teaspoon ground ginger

½ teaspoon ground cloves

DOUGH

1⅓ cups gluten-free all-purpose flour,
  plus extra for dusting

3 tablespoons rice flour

2 tablespoons vegan and gluten-free
  confectioners' sugar

½ teaspoon xanthan gum

pinch of salt

½ cup firmly packed vegan and gluten-
  free margarine

vegan and gluten-free egg replacer,
  equivalent to 1 egg

1 To make the filling, steam the pumpkin for 25 minutes, or until tender. Let cool a little, then transfer to the bowl of a food processor with the remaining filling ingredients and process to a thick cream. Alternatively, if using the canned pumpkin puree, process in the food processor with the remaining ingredients to a thick cream. Preheat the oven to 350°F.

2 To make the dough, put the flours, confectioners' sugar, xanthan gum, and salt into a large mixing bowl and mix together with a wooden spoon. Rub in the margarine with your fingertips. Make up the egg replacer in a small bowl according to the package directions, and beat it with a fork for a minute, until bubbly. Stir in the egg replacer and enough cold water to bring the mixture together to form a dough.

3 Turn out the dough onto a lightly floured work surface and shape into a firm ball. Roll out the dough to about ⅛ inch thick and use it to line a 9-inch round fluted tart pan.

4 Pour the filling into the pastry crust and smooth the top with a spatula. Bake in the preheated oven for 50 minutes. Let the pie cool in the pan for 10 minutes before serving or serve cold.

Cook's tip

The filling of this pie will still look soft when it comes out of the oven, but don't worry—the filling will become firm as it cools.

3

3

6

Pecan & Cranberry PIE

This traditional dessert is so delicious it could hold its own in any competition for the best American fruit pie.

1 For the filling, put the cranberries in a small bowl with the orange juice and brandy, if using. Set aside for at least an hour to plump up.

2 Preheat the oven to 375°F.

3 To make the dough, rub the margarine into the flour in a large mixing bowl and then stir in the xanthan gum and confectioners' sugar. Gradually add enough cold water to make a soft dough. Roll the dough out on a floured work surface and use it to line an 8-inch tart pan. Put the pecans into the pastry crust and bake in the preheated oven for 15 minutes.

4 Put the maple syrup, soy milk, vanilla extract, cinnamon, ginger, and orange zest into a medium saucepan over low heat. Simmer gently for 5 minutes, then remove from the heat.

5 Remove the pastry crust from the oven but leave the oven on. Use a slotted spoon to remove the cranberries from the soaking liquid and arrange them on top of the pecans. Stir the flaxseed meal into the remaining soaking liquid and then stir this into the maple mixture. Carefully pour the maple mixture into the pastry crust.

6 Return the pie to the oven for an additional 30 minutes. Let cool before slicing and serving.

DOUGH

¼ cup firmly packed vegan and gluten-free margarine

1¼ cups gluten-free all-purpose flour, plus extra for dusting

½ teaspoon xanthan gum

2 tablespoons vegan and gluten-free confectioners' sugar

FILLING

¼ cup dried cranberries

zest and juice of 1 unwaxed orange

1 tablespoon vegan brandy (optional)

1¼ cups pecans

⅔ cup maple syrup

½ cup gluten-free soy milk

3 tablespoons vanilla extract

1 teaspoon ground cinnamon

1 teaspoon ground ginger

1 teaspoon flaxseed meal

White Chocolate & Raspberry TARTS

These fresh and fruity raspberry tarts with a smooth white chocolate filling are delicious and great for dinner parties.

1 Preheat the oven to 350°F.

2 To make the dough, make up the egg replacer in a small bowl according to the package directions, and beat it with a fork for a minute, until bubbly. Put the flour, confectioners' sugar, xanthan gum, and salt into a large mixing bowl and mix together with a wooden spoon. Rub in the margarine with your fingertips. Stir in the egg replacer and use your hands to bring the mixture together in a soft ball.

3 Transfer the dough to a lightly floured work surface and cut it into six equal pieces. Roll each piece out to line six shallow 4-inch round, loose-bottom individual tart pans.

4 Bake the tart crusts in the preheated oven for 7–10 minutes, or until just firm but not browning, then set aside to cool.

5 To make the filling, put the margarine and sugar into a small saucepan and heat gently, stirring, until the margarine has melted and the sugar has dissolved. Put the cornstarch into a small bowl and mix to a smooth paste with a little of the soy milk. Add the chocolate to the saucepan with the remaining soy milk. Heat gently, stirring, until the chocolate has melted. Remove the saucepan from the heat, add the cornstarch paste and vanilla, and beat with a whisk for 1 minute, or until the mixture is thick and smooth. Spoon the filling into the pastry crusts and let cool, then transfer to a refrigerator and chill for 30 minutes.

6 Just before serving, cut the raspberries in half and arrange them on top of the tarts. Dust with a little confectioners' sugar, if desired.

DOUGH

vegan and gluten-free egg replacer, equivalent to 2 eggs

1¼ cups gluten-free all-purpose flour, plus extra for dusting

3 tablespoons vegan and gluten-free confectioners' sugar

1½ teaspoons xanthan gum

pinch of salt

⅓ cup firmly packed vegan and gluten-free margarine

FILLING

¼ cup firmly packed vegan and gluten-free margarine

¼ cup vegan superfine or granulated sugar

1 tablespoon gluten-free cornstarch

1⅓ cups gluten-free soy milk

2 ounces vegan and gluten-free white chocolate, broken into pieces

1 teaspoon vanilla extract

TOPPING

½ cup raspberries

vegan and gluten-free confectioners' sugar, for dusting (optional)

Pear & Hazelnut TART

There are several steps to this recipe, but each one is easy, and they add up to a very impressive tart.

1 Put the hazelnuts into the bowl of a food processor fitted with a chopping blade and process until finely chopped. Add the brown sugar and margarine and process for an additional minute, until the mixture comes together as a soft dough. Form the dough into a ball, wrap with plastic wrap, and put into the refrigerator to chill for at least 30 minutes.

2 Preheat the oven to 300°F. Grease a 7-inch springform cake pan. Put the superfine sugar into a large saucepan with 3 tablespoons of water and heat it gently, stirring occasionally, for 1 minute, or until the sugar has dissolved and the liquid is clear. Slice the pear in half from top to bottom, then cut each half lengthwise into three slices of equal thickness. Arrange the pear slices in the saucepan and increase the heat so that the sugar syrup bubbles gently. Cook the pears in the syrup, turning occasionally, for 5 minutes, or until the pear is soft and the syrup is reduced and sticky. Let the pears sit in the saucepan to cool.

3 Take the hazelnut dough out of the refrigerator and use your fingers to press it into the prepared pan. Press the dough down firmly and make sure the bottom is covered. Bring the dough up the sides of the pan to form a pie crust about 1½ inches deep. Bake in the preheated oven for 15 minutes, then set aside to cool.

4 To make the filling, put the superfine sugar and margarine into a large saucepan. Heat gently to melt the margarine. Put the cornstarch into a small bowl and add enough soy milk to make a smooth paste. Pour the rest of the soy milk into the saucepan and bring to boiling point. Reduce the heat to low and whisk in the cornstarch mixture and vanilla. Keep whisking until the mixture thickens—this will take about 3 minutes. The consistency should be like a thick custard (too thick to pour). Let the filling to cool for 5 minutes, then carefully spoon it into the hazelnut crust and smooth the surface with a spatula. Carefully arrange the pear slices on top, pressing them down gently so that the surface of the pears is at the same level as the surface of the filling. Chill, then serve with a sprinkle of brown sugar.

DOUGH

1⅓ cups toasted hazelnuts, chopped

2 tablespoons packed vegan light brown sugar, plus 3 tablespoons to serve

2 tablespoons packed vegan and gluten-free margarine, plus extra for greasing

PEAR SLICES

2 tablespoons vegan superfine or granulated sugar

1 large unwaxed Bosc pear

FILLING

¼ cup vegan superfine or granulated sugar

¼ cup firmly packed vegan and gluten-free margarine

⅓ cup gluten-free cornstarch

1⅓ cups gluten-free soy milk

1 teaspoon vanilla extract

Plum FRANGIPANE

This is a large, decorative tart that is ideal for entertaining or for serving at family dinners.

1 Preheat the oven to 350°F. Make up the egg replacers for both the dough and the filling in two separate small bowls according to the package directions, and beat them with a fork for a minute, until bubbly.

2 To make the dough, put the flour, confectioners' sugar, xanthan gum, and salt into a large mixing bowl and mix together with a wooden spoon. Rub in the margarine with your fingertips. Stir in the egg replacer and enough cold water to bring the mixture together to form a dough.

3 Turn out the dough onto a lightly floured work surface and shape it into a firm ball. Roll the dough out to about ⅛ inch thick and use it to line a 10-inch round, fluted tart pan. Bake the pastry crust for 10 minutes, then set aside to cool.

4 To make the filling, cream together the margarine, sugar, egg replacer, amaretto, and vanilla extract with a wooden spoon in a large mixing bowl. Mix in the flour and ground almonds.

5 Spoon the filling into the pastry crust and smooth the top with a spatula. Bake in the preheated oven for 25–30 minutes, or until the top is golden. Set aside to cool and firm.

6 Put the apricot preserves into a small saucepan with a tablespoon of water. Bring to a boil, stirring constantly, then pass through a fine-mesh strainer and let cool a little. Arrange the plums on top of the tart and pour the apricot glaze over the top. Let cool slightly before serving.

DOUGH

vegan and gluten-free egg replacer, equivalent to 2 eggs

1¼ cups gluten-free all-purpose flour, plus extra for dusting

¼ cup vegan and gluten-free confectioners' sugar

1½ teaspoons xanthan gum

pinch of salt

⅓ cup firmly packed vegan and gluten-free margarine

FILLING

vegan and gluten-free egg replacer, equivalent to 3 eggs

½ cup firmly packed vegan and gluten-free margarine

⅔ cup vegan superfine or granulated sugar

1 tablespoon vegan amaretto

1 teaspoon vanilla extract

2 tablespoons gluten-free all-purpose flour

¾ cup ground almonds

TOPPING

½ cup gluten-free, unwaxed apricot preserves

2½ cups pitted and sliced, unwaxed red-skinned plums

Ginger Ice Cream PIE

*Chopped preserved ginger adds some sophistication to a pie
that's real comfort food.*

1 Crush the gingersnaps to fine crumbs using a food processor or put them into a sealed plastic food bag, lay the bag on a cutting board, and break up the cookies with a rolling pin. Set aside 3 tablespoons of the crushed cookies to use as the topping for the pie.

2 Put the rest of the crushed cookies into a large mixing bowl with the coconut oil, maple syrup, and ginger syrup, and stir together with a wooden spoon until well combined.

3 Pour the cookie mixture into an 8-inch round, loose-bottom cake pan. Use the tips of your fingers to press it into a smooth layer covering the bottom of the pan.

4 Warm the chocolate nut spread a little, either in a small bowl in the microwave, using short 30-second spurts, or in a small saucepan on the stove, so that it softens and becomes easier to spread. Carefully spoon it into the pan and use the back of a spoon or a rubber spatula to spread it over the crumb crust.

5 Place the crumb crust in the freezer for at least an hour until firm.

6 Take the ice cream out of the freezer and let it soften at room temperature for about 15 minutes, or until it is soft enough to mash but not completely runny. Put the softened ice cream into a large mixing bowl. Stir the preserved ginger into the ice cream, making sure it is well dispersed.

7 Take the crumb crust out of the freezer and fill it with the ice cream. Smooth the top and sprinkle over the reserved crushed ginger cookies. Return to the freezer for at least an hour before serving. To serve, lift the pie out of the pan, place on a plate, and let soften at room temperature for a few minutes before cutting into slices.

10½ ounces vegan and gluten-free gingersnaps (about 2½ cups when crushed)

2 tablespoons coconut oil

2 tablespoons maple syrup

1 tablespoon ginger syrup from a jar of preserved ginger

½ cup vegan and gluten-free chocolate nut spread

3 cups vegan and gluten-free vanilla ice cream

2 pieces of preserved ginger, finely chopped

Cook's tip

The chocolate spread layer can be omitted if you can't obtain this ingredient—or use a thin layer of melted vegan and gluten-free semisweet chocolate instead.

Raw Fruit TART

This quick and easy fruit tart is a guilt-free treat—try it for breakfast!

1 Soak the cashew nuts for the cashew cream in a bowl of water for approximately 8 hours or overnight.

2 Put all the ingredients for the tart crust into the bowl of a food processor fitted with a chopping blade. Process until the nuts are finely chopped and the mixture begins to clump together. Press the dough into the bottom of an 8-inch pie plate and use the back of a spoon to smooth it into a firm crust.

3 To make the mixed fruit topping, hull and halve or quarter strawberries, halve grapes or blackberries, and core and chop apples or pears. Put the prepared fruit into a large mixing bowl and toss with the lemon juice and vanilla extract. Arrange the fruit over the tart crust.

4 To make the cashew cream, drain the soaked cashews and put them into the bowl of a food processor fitted with a chopping blade. Add the agave nectar, lemon juice, and ¾ cup of cold water. Blend to a smooth cream and serve immediately with the tart.

CRUST

1½ cups pecans

½ cup pitted, unwaxed dates

1 teaspoon ground cinnamon

1 tablespoon vanilla extract

a pinch of salt

TOPPING

8 ounces mixed fresh unwaxed fruit (choose a colorful selection of fresh fruit in season; about ½ cup prepared)

juice of ½ an unwaxed lemon

1 tablespoon vanilla extract

CASHEW CREAM

1¾ cups cashew nuts

1 tablespoon agave nectar

1 tablespoon unwaxed lemon juice

Cook's tip

Soaking the cashew nuts makes the cream less grainy, but you can skip the soaking if you forget to do it ahead of time (it will still be good).

1

3

4

Rhubarb & Custard TARTS

Rhubarb and custard is a retro combination that's back in fashion—a delectable mixture of sweet and creamy with tart and tangy!

1 Place the rhubarb into a small saucepan with the sugar and 3 tablespoons of water. Cook over medium heat for 3–4 minutes, stirring frequently, until the rhubarb has disintegrated. Set aside to cool.

2 Make up the custard or vanilla pie filling following the package directions. Set aside to cool. Make up the egg replacer in a small bowl according to the package directions, and beat it with a fork for a minute, until bubbly. Preheat the oven to 325°F.

3 To make the dough, put the flour, confectioners' sugar, and xanthan gum into a large mixing bowl and stir with a wooden spoon to combine. Rub in the margarine with your fingertips, then gradually stir in the egg replacer and use your hands to bring the mixture together in a soft ball.

4 Transfer the dough to a lightly floured work surface and cut it into six equal pieces. Roll each piece out to line six shallow 4-inch round, loose-bottom individual tart pans.

5 Bake the tart shells in the preheated oven for 7–10 minutes, or until just firm but not browning, then remove from the oven and fill with the cooled custard or vanilla pie filling. Swirl two or three teaspoons of rhubarb into each tart.

6 Return the tarts to the oven and bake for 10 more minutes, or until the filling is just golden. Serve warm or cold.

1¼ cups chopped fresh rhubarb

2½ tablespoons vegan granulated sugar

2 cups custard (made with vegan and gluten-free custard powder or vanilla pie filling mix and soy milk)

DOUGH

vegan and gluten-free egg replacer, equivalent to 2 eggs

1¼ cups gluten-free all-purpose flour, plus extra for dusting

¼ cup vegan and gluten-free confectioners' sugar

1½ teaspoons xanthan gum

⅓ cup firmly packed vegan and gluten-free margarine

Cook's tip

It's best to start from scratch with custard powder or vanilla pie filling mix because prepared custard or vanilla pudding does not work well in tarts.

Chocolate & Banana CREAM PIE

With bananas, cashew nuts, and chocolate all used in this recipe, it makes a great showcase for a range of tasty ingredients!

CRUST

1¼ cups cashew nuts

2 tablespoons packed vegan light brown sugar

¼ cup vegan and gluten-free unsweetened cocoa powder

2 tablespoons packed vegan and gluten-free margarine, plus extra for greasing

BANANA CREAM

1 cup cashew nuts

12 ounces extra firm silken tofu

½ cup vegan superfine or granulated sugar

2 tablespoons unwaxed lemon juice

2 tablespoons coconut oil

2 very ripe unwaxed bananas (about 6 ounces)

pinch of salt

CHOCOLATE ICING

2 ounces vegan and gluten-free semisweet chocolate, broken into pieces

2 tablespoons coconut milk

½ teaspoon vanilla extract

dried vegan banana chips, to decorate (optional)

1 Grease a 7-inch springform cake pan.

2 To make the crust, put the cashew nuts into a heavy skillet and heat them gently, stirring frequently, for 2–3 minutes, or until they begin to turn golden. Let cool, then transfer to the bowl of a food processor fitted with a chopping blade and process until finely chopped. Add the sugar, cocoa powder, and margarine and process for an additional minute, until the mixture comes together as a soft dough. Form the dough into a ball, wrap it with plastic wrap, and place in the refrigerator to chill for at least 30 minutes. Preheat the oven to 300°F.

3 Take the cashew dough out of the refrigerator and use your fingers to press it into the prepared pan. Press the dough down firmly. Bring the dough up the sides of the pan to form a pie crust about 1½ inches deep. Bake in the preheated oven for 15 minutes, then set aside to cool.

4 To make the banana cream, put the cashew nuts into the bowl of a food processor fitted with a chopping blade and process to a fine powder. Add the remaining ingredients and process to a smooth, thick cream. Spoon the banana cream into the pie crust, smooth the top, and refrigerate for at least an hour.

5 To make the chocolate icing, put the chocolate and coconut milk into a double boiler or a heatproof bowl set over a saucepan of gently simmering water and melt together, stirring frequently with a metal spoon. Stir in the vanilla extract. Remove the bowl from the heat and beat the mixture with a metal fork until glossy and smooth.

6 Take the pie out of the refrigerator, spoon the warm chocolate icing over the top, quickly smooth it with a rubber spatula, and decorate with banana chips, if using. Return the pie to the refrigerator to chill for at least another hour before loosening the sides of the pan and transferring to a plate to serve.

Cook's tip

Don't be tempted to cut back on the chilling time in this recipe, because the pie needs to be completely chilled in order to be sure that it holds its shape when it is sliced.

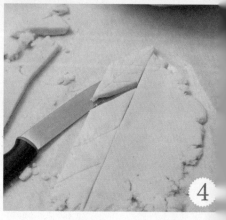

Apple & Cinnamon PIE

A fall or winter classic, this is a generous showstopper dessert for finishing off any family meal or dinner party.

1 To make the dough, put the vegetable shortening and margarine into a large mixing bowl. Pour ½ cup of boiling water over the top and mix with a wooden spoon until creamy. Add the flour, baking powder, and salt, stir together, then turn out onto a lightly floured work surface and knead together into a smooth ball. Let the dough cool for 5 minutes. Roll the dough out on a sheet of plastic wrap to a shape that slightly overhangs a 9-inch round pie plate. Set aside.

2 Preheat the oven to 350°F.

3 Place the apples in a large saucepan with the sugar, cornstarch, and cinnamon, and add 3 tablespoons of water. Cook gently for 5–10 minutes, or until the apple is just tender and most of the liquid in the pan has been thickened by the cornstarch. Let the mixture cool.

4 Put the apple filling into the pie plate. Lift the dough on the sheet of plastic wrap (to support it) and carefully transfer to the top of the pie, pressing the edges down to form a seal and trimming away any excess with a sharp knife. Reroll the scraps to make decorative leaves and place these on top of the pie.

5 Brush the top of the pie with a little soy milk and sprinkle with a little sugar. Bake in the preheated oven for 30 minutes, or until just golden. Serve hot or cold.

DOUGH

⅓ cup firmly packed vegetable shortening

1 tablespoon packed vegan and gluten-free margarine

1¾ cups gluten-free all-purpose flour, plus extra for dusting

1 tablespoon gluten-free baking powder

pinch of salt

gluten-free soy milk, for brushing

FILLING

7 unwaxed cooking apples, such as Granny Smiths (about 2¼ pounds), peeled, cored, and sliced

¾ cup vegan granulated sugar, plus extra for sprinkling

2 teaspoons gluten-free cornstarch

1 tablespoon ground cinnamon

Cook's tip
Precooking the apples removes some of the water that could otherwise make the pastry soggy.

Mango CHEESECAKE

This is a rich dessert, but lightened by the fresh flavor of the sliced mango topping and filling.

CRUST

⅓ cup firmly packed vegan and gluten-free margarine, plus extra for greasing

1½ cups crushed vegan and gluten-free cookies

⅓ cup ground almonds

FILLING

1 large unwaxed mango, pitted, peeled, and diced

juice of 1 unwaxed lemon

1 cup gluten-free soy yogurt

1 tablespoon gluten-free cornstarch

3 tablespoons maple syrup

2 cups vegan and gluten-free cream cheese

TOPPING

3 tablespoons maple syrup

1 small unwaxed mango, pitted, peeled, and sliced

1 Preheat the oven to 350°F. Lightly grease a 9-inch round, loose-bottom cake pan.

2 To make the cookie crust, melt the margarine in a saucepan, then stir in the crushed cookies and almonds with a wooden spoon. Press the dough into the bottom of the prepared cake pan to make an even layer. Bake in the preheated oven for 10 minutes.

3 Meanwhile, to make the filling, put the mango, lemon juice, yogurt, cornstarch, maple syrup, and cream cheese into a food processor or blender and process until smooth. Pour the mixture over the cookie crust and smooth the surface.

4 Bake for 25–30 minutes, or until golden and set. Let cool in the pan, then transfer to a wire rack and chill in the refrigerator for 30 minutes.

5 To make the topping, heat the maple syrup in a saucepan. Brush the top of the cheesecake with some of the maple syrup. Add the mango to the remaining maple syrup in the pan and cook for 1 minute, stirring. Let cool slightly, then arrange the mango slices on top of the cheesecake. Pour over any remaining syrup before serving.

Cook's tip
This cheesecake also tastes great with fresh unwaxed passion fruit drizzled over the top.

Cook's tip

Acidic fruit will melt vegan gelatins, so decorate your cheesecake with grated semisweet chocolate instead.

PREP TIME: 25 minutes, plus chilling

COOK TIME: None

SERVES: 8

Lemon Gelatin CHEESECAKE

This is an unusual but delicious cheesecake, with a crispy rice crust and smooth lemony topping.

1 Line an 8-inch round, springform cake pan with aluminum foil, letting the foil extend beyond the edges of the pan.

2 Crush or chop the rice cakes into fine pieces, or process them briefly in a food processor so that they still have some texture. Melt the chocolate and hazelnut butter together in a double boiler or a heatproof bowl set over a small saucepan of gently simmering water. Put the crushed rice cakes into a large mixing bowl, pour in the chocolate mixture, and stir until all the rice pieces are coated with chocolate.

3 Put the mixture into the prepared pan and press it down with the back of a spoon. Chill in the refrigerator for 30 minutes, until the chocolate has set.

4 Make 2½ cups of lemon gelatin following the package directions. Let the mixture cool in a small bowl, but don't let it set. When the mixture is cool, pour it into the bowl of a food processor, add the cream cheese, and process until smooth. Alternatively, beat them together in a large mixing bowl.

5 Pour the gelatin mixture over the top of the rice crust. Put the cheesecake back into the refrigerator for 2 hours, or until completely set. To serve, carefully release the sides of the pan and use the foil for support as you transfer it to a serving plate. Decorate with grated chocolate, if desired.

3 gluten-free rice cakes

3 ounces vegan and gluten-free semisweet chocolate, broken into pieces, plus extra grated chocolate to decorate (optional)

2 tablespoons vegan hazelnut butter

TOPPING

1 (3-ounce) envelope vegan and gluten-free lemon gelatin crystals or vegan and gluten-free dessert mix in a flavor of your choice

1½ cups vegan and gluten-free cream cheese

Pear & Cardamom CHEESECAKE

The crust of this cheesecake is made with crushed rice cakes, which gives it a wonderfully crispy and chewy texture.

1 Preheat the oven to 350°F. Grease an 8-inch springform cake pan and line with parchment paper.

2 Put the dates into a small saucepan with ⅓ cup of water over low heat. Heat gently and simmer for 5 minutes, or until they are softening into the water. Stir in the coconut oil and melt the oil into the date mixture. Crush the rice cakes finely—a food processor is best for this but you could also use a rolling pin. Stir the crushed rice cakes and dry unsweetened coconut into the date mixture and mix together thoroughly.

3 Spoon the crust mixture into the prepared pan and use the back of a metal spoon to press it down firmly, making a smooth layer to cover the bottom of the pan.

4 To make the filling, put all the ingredients, except the pears, into the bowl of a food processor fitted with a chopping blade and process until smooth and creamy. Fold the chopped pears into the mixture. Spoon the filling into the pan and smooth the top with a rubber spatula. Bake in the preheated oven for 45–50 minutes, or until beginning to brown. The cheesecake should still be wobbly when you take it out of the oven. Let cool at room temperature and then put it into the refrigerator for at least 2 hours to chill and set.

5 To make the pear chips, preheat the oven to 275°F. Put the sugar and lemon juice into a small saucepan with 1 tablespoon of water and warm gently to dissolve the sugar. Remove the pan from the heat and carefully dip each pear slice into the sugar solution, then place the slices on a baking pan lined with parchment paper. Bake in the preheated oven for 1 hour, or until crisp and golden, then carefully transfer to a clean sheet of parchment paper to cool. Decorate the cheesecake with the pear chips just before serving.

CRUST

vegan and gluten-free margarine, for greasing

⅓ cup chopped, pitted unwaxed dates

2 teaspoons coconut oil

3 gluten-free rice cakes

½ cup dry unsweetened coconut

FILLING

12 ounces extra firm silken tofu

1 cup vegan and gluten-free cream cheese

2½ tablespoons vegan superfine or granulated sugar

¼ cup gluten-free all-purpose flour

¼ teaspoon xanthan gum

1 teaspoon ground cardamom

pinch of salt

¼ teaspoon gluten-free baking soda

2 unwaxed Bosc pears, peeled, cored, and finely chopped

PEAR CHIPS

2 tablespoons vegan superfine or granulated sugar

1 tablespoon unwaxed lemon juice

1 unwaxed Bosc pear, cored and thinly sliced

Rhubarb & Blackberry CRISP

This is a classic winter warmer that is so comforting it will banish away the cold weather blues.

1 Preheat the oven to 350°F. Grease a 9-inch ovenproof dish.

2 Put the rhubarb into a baking pan, sprinkle with the superfine sugar, and roast in the oven for 12–15 minutes.

3 When cooked, put the rhubarb into the prepared dish with the blackberries, vanilla extract, and ginger. Stir well to combine.

4 For the topping, rub the margarine and flour together with your fingertips until the mixture resembles fine bread crumbs. Add the demerara sugar and almonds and mix together. Cover the rhubarb mixture with the crumb topping and bake in the preheated oven for 35–40 minutes, until golden. Serve immediately.

8–10 rhubarb stalks, cut into bite-size pieces (about 1¾ pounds)

½ cup vegan superfine or granulated sugar

2 cups blackberries

½ teaspoon vanilla extract

½ teaspoon ground ginger

CRUMB TOPPING

½ cup firmly packed vegan and gluten-free margarine, plus extra for greasing

1⅔ cups gluten-free all-purpose flour

½ cup vegan demerara or other raw brown sugar

2 tablespoons slivered almonds

Pear & Apple
OAT CRISP

With its classic winter-spiced flavors, this easy dessert makes a great alternative to heavy, pastry-base pies on blustery, cold days.

1 Preheat the oven to 325°F. Grease a medium rectangular baking dish.

2 Put the apple, pear, apple juice, cornstarch, cinnamon, agave, and cloves in a large bowl. Stir well with a wooden spoon to combine.

3 To make the crumb mixture, mix the flour, sugar, walnuts, oats, and margarine in a large bowl, rubbing the ingredients together with your fingertips.

4 Spread a small layer of crumb mixture over the bottom of the prepared baking dish. Arrange the apple-and-pear mixture on top, and sprinkle with the remaining crumb mixture.

5 Bake in the preheated oven for 30–35 minutes, until golden brown and crisp on top. Serve immediately.

3 unwaxed cooking apples, such as Granny Smiths, peeled, cored, and sliced

3 unwaxed Bosc pears, peeled, cored, and sliced

3 teaspoons unwaxed apple juice

½ teaspoon gluten-free cornstarch

½ teaspoon ground cinnamon

2 tablespoons agave syrup

2 cloves

OAT CRUMB MIXTURE

½ cup gluten-free all-purpose flour

½ cup firmly packed vegan light brown sugar

3 tablespoons chopped walnuts

⅔ cup gluten-free rolled oats

½ cup firmly packed vegan and gluten-free margarine, plus extra for greasing

2

3

4

Cook's tip

This crisp is great with vegan and gluten-free ice cream or coconut whipped cream.

Cook's tip

Store-bought granola is already baked, so it doesn't need long in the oven.

Summer Fruit
GRANOLA CRISP

This makes a fabulous breakfast or a great summer dessert, with the fresh and fruity flavors combining deliciously with the crunchy granola.

1 Preheat the oven to 350°F.

2 Put the strawberries, raspberries, and blueberries into a large mixing bowl. Add the lemon juice, sugar, and cornstarch and stir to mix the ingredients thoroughly. Transfer the fruit to a deep baking dish about 6 x 9 inches in size. Bake, uncovered, in the preheated oven for 15 minutes, or until the fruit is softened.

3 Sprinkle the granola over the fruit and bake the dish for an additional 10 minutes. Serve immediately.

8 ounces strawberries, hulled, halved or quartered if large

1⅔ cups raspberries

1⅓ cups blueberries

juice of ½ an unwaxed lemon

2 tablespoons vegan superfine or granulated sugar

1 tablespoon gluten-free cornstarch

1⅔ cups vegan and gluten-free granola

Chili Chocolate CAKES
with Chili Chocolate SAUCE

This combination of spicy chili powder and decadently rich chocolate is a real winter warmer and makes a great dessert for entertaining.

1 Preheat the oven to 300°F. Grease four ovenproof ramekins (individual ceramic dishes) and line with parchment paper.

2 Cream together the margarine and maple syrup with a wooden spoon. Add the flour, cocoa powder, baking powder, ground almonds, and chili powder and mix thoroughly. Divide the batter evenly among the ramekins.

3 Place the ramekins in a small baking pan and bake in the preheated oven for 40 minutes, or until firm and springy to the touch. Let cool slightly, then turn out onto serving plates.

4 To make the sauce, break the chocolate into small pieces and place in a small saucepan with the sugar, soy cream, and ¼ cup of boiling water. Heat gently to melt the chocolate and stir together thoroughly. Add the chili powder, according to your taste. Pour the sauce over the cakes, then serve immediately.

⅓ cup firmly packed vegan and gluten-free margarine, plus extra for greasing

¼ cup maple syrup

⅓ cup gluten-free all-purpose flour

3 tablespoons vegan and gluten-free unsweetened cocoa powder

½ teaspoon gluten-free baking powder

⅔ cup ground almonds

pinch of chili powder

SAUCE

8 ounces vegan and gluten-free semisweet chocolate

⅓ cup vegan superfine or granulated sugar

½ cup gluten-free soy cream

pinch of chili powder

Cook's tip
More subtle spices, such as cinnamon and ground ginger, also work well in this recipe.

Cook's tip

Try adding 2 tablespoons of chopped candied peel or use almond extract in place of vanilla.

Date & Pistachio CAKES

These are pure comfort food, especially when these individual cakes are served hot on a blustery evening.

1 Preheat the oven to 300°F. Grease four ovenproof ramekins (individual ceramic dishes) and line with parchment paper.

2 Place the pistachios and dates into a small mixing bowl and mix together with the margarine. Divide the mixture among the ramekins.

3 To make the cakes, cream together the margarine and maple syrup with a wooden spoon. Add the flour, baking powder, ground almonds, and vanilla and mix thoroughly. Divide the batter among the ramekins.

4 Place the ramekins in a small baking pan and bake in the preheated oven for 40 minutes, or until golden and springy to the touch. Turn out onto serving plates and drizzle with warmed maple syrup before serving.

⅓ cup firmly packed vegan and gluten-free margarine, plus extra for greasing

¼ cup maple syrup

⅓ cup gluten-free all-purpose flour

½ teaspoon gluten-free baking powder

⅔ cup ground almonds

½ teaspoon vanilla extract

maple syrup, to serve

TOPPING

½ cup shelled pistachio nuts, finely chopped

⅔ cup finely chopped, pitted, unwaxed dates

2 tablespoons packed vegan and gluten-free margarine

CHAPTER 5

Savory

Seeded BREAD LOAF

This is an easy, wholesome loaf, which is best eaten on the day that it is made.

1 Put the flour, salt, yeast, and sugar into a large mixing bowl and stir them together with a wooden spoon. Put the seeds into a small bowl, mix well, and set aside 1 tablespoon to be used as the topping.

2 Make up the egg replacer in a small bowl according to the package directions, and beat it with a fork for a minute, until bubbly. In a large bowl, mix together the soy milk, vinegar, oil, and egg replacer.

3 Add the seeds and wet ingredients to the flour. Mix well with a wooden spoon to form a sticky dough.

4 Place the dough into an oiled 9 x 5 x 3-inch loaf pan and use a spatula to push it into the corners and smooth the top. Cover with oiled plastic wrap and let rest in a warm place for 1 hour.

5 Preheat the oven to 425°F.

6 Brush the surface of the loaf with a little soy milk and sprinkle the reserved seed mixture over the top. Bake in the center of the preheated oven for 40–45 minutes, or until browned and baked through. Let cool in the pan before turning out and slicing.

3–3½ cups gluten-free multigrain bread flour or gluten-free bread flour mix (1 pound in weight)

½ teaspoon salt

2 teaspoons active dry yeast

2 tablespoons vegan brown sugar

1 tablespoon pumpkin seeds

1 tablespoon poppy seeds

1 tablespoon sunflower seeds

vegan and gluten-free egg replacer, equivalent to 2 eggs

1½ cups gluten-free soy milk, plus extra for brushing

1 teaspoon vegan and gluten-free cider vinegar

⅓ cup canola oil, plus extra for greasing

Cook's tip

If using a bread flour mix, check the package directions and adjust the recipe, if necessary. The bread does not rise much in step 4, but giving the yeast some time to work improves the texture and taste of the bread.

Cook's tip

You can vary the types of
dried fruit included in
this recipe to suit your
personal tastes.

PREP TIME: 20 minutes, plus standing

COOK TIME: 25-30 minutes

MAKES: 1 loaf

Fruit Soda BREAD

This is a different take on the standard Irish soda bread and is full of dried fruit flavors.

- ⅓ cup chopped, pitted unwaxed prunes
- ½ cup ready-to-eat chopped, dried unwaxed apricots
- ½ cup chopped, dried unwaxed apples
- ¼ cup dried cranberries
- ⅔ cup unwaxed apple juice
- 3½ cups gluten-free all-purpose flour
- 1½ tablespoons gluten-free baking powder
- 2 teaspoons xanthan gum
- ¼ teaspoon salt
- 2 tablespoons sunflower oil, plus extra for greasing
- 1 cup gluten-free soy milk, plus extra for brushing
- ¼ cup maple syrup
- 1 tablespoon pumpkin seeds

1 Put the prunes, apricots, apples, and cranberries in a bowl and pour the apple juice over the fruit. Cover and let stand for about 30 minutes.

2 Preheat the oven to 400°F. Brush a baking pan with oil. Sift the flour, baking powder, xanthan gum, and salt into a bowl and make a well in the center. Mix the oil, milk, and maple syrup and add to the well in the dry ingredients with the fruits and juice, mixing lightly to a soft, but not sticky, dough. Add a little more milk if the dough feels dry.

3 Shape the dough to a smooth round on the prepared baking pan, flatten slightly, and cut a deep cross through the center almost to the bottom. Gently pull the wedges apart at the points. Brush with milk and sprinkle with pumpkin seeds.

4 Bake in the preheated oven for 25–30 minutes, or until golden brown and the bottom sounds hollow when tapped.

Cook's tip

Experiment with hard vegan and gluten-free cheeses—you may find a blue cheese which works well in this recipe. Soft vegan and gluten-free cheese will make the bread too wet.

Cheese & Chive BREAD

This soda bread-style loaf uses soy yogurt in place of buttermilk.
Try it sliced and toasted with a steaming bowl of soup.

1 Preheat the oven to 350°F. Grease a 7-inch round, springform cake pan and line with parchment paper.

2 Sift the flour and baking powder into a large mixing bowl and stir in the xanthan gum and flaxseed meal with a wooden spoon.

3 Make up the egg replacer in a small bowl according to the package directions, and beat it with a fork for a minute, until bubbly. Add it to the flour mixture, along with the coconut oil and soy yogurt, and stir well to combine.

4 Fold the chives and shredded cheese into the dough and spoon into the prepared pan. Smooth the top with a rubber spatula or leave it rough if you prefer a more rustic look.

5 Bake in the preheated oven for 45–50 minutes, or until a toothpick inserted into the center of the loaf comes out clean. Let cool in the pan for 5 minutes, then release the sides of the pan and transfer the bread to a wire rack to cool before slicing.

vegan and gluten-free margarine, for greasing

1½ cups gluten-free white bread flour

4 teaspoons gluten-free baking powder

½ teaspoon xanthan gum

3 tablespoons flaxseed meal

vegan and gluten-free egg replacer, equivalent to 3 eggs

¼ cup coconut oil

1¼ cups gluten-free soy yogurt

½ cup snipped fresh chives

1 cup shredded vegan and gluten-free cheddar-style cheese

Italian Chickpea BREAD

This traditional Italian bread, made with chickpea flour, is perfect for mopping up a rich tomato sauce.

1 Put the flour into a large mixing bowl. Gradually whisk in 3½ cups of cold water using a wire whisk or a handheld electric mixer. Whisk the mixture until it is completely smooth and then season with salt and pepper. Set the bowl aside for 3 hours to let the batter to thicken.

2 Preheat the oven to 350°F.

3 Put the oil into a 13- x 9-inch baking pan with a rim of at least ½ inch.

4 Give the batter a quick stir with a wooden spoon and pour it into the baking pan to form a layer that is about ¼ inch thick. Arrange the rosemary sprigs in a decorative pattern on top of the batter.

5 Carefully put the baking pan into the preheated oven. A steady hand is useful because the oil underneath the wet batter tends to make it slide about in the pan. Bake for 35–40 minutes, or until golden brown and firm. Let cool for 5 minutes in the pan before slicing.

2½ cups chickpea (besan) flour
¼ cup extra virgin olive oil
salt and pepper, to taste
sprigs of fresh rosemary, to garnish

Mexican-Style
TORTILLA WRAPS

These Mexican flour tortilla wraps can be used for lunchtime wraps or for burrito or fajita dishes.

1 Mix the yeast, lukewarm water, and oil in a small bowl and let rest at room temperature for about 20 minutes, until frothy.

2 Sift the flour and xanthan gum into a large bowl and make a well in the center. Add the yeast liquid to the well slowly with the cilantro and red pepper flakes, if using, and season with salt and pepper. Mix well to form a sticky dough.

3 Turn out onto a floured surface and knead well. Divide into ten balls.

4 Cut out a circle of parchment paper 8 inches in diameter and roll out each ball of dough under this, the thinner the better.

5 Place a large skillet over medium heat. Add the tortillas to the pan, one at a time, and cook for 2–3 minutes, or until bubbling and turning golden brown. Flip over and cook the other side for 2–3 minutes, or until golden brown. Serve hot or cold with your favorite fillings.

3¼ teaspoons active dry yeast

1⅔ cups lukewarm water

2 tablespoons sunflower oil

3 cups gluten-free all-purpose flour, plus extra for dusting

1½ teaspoons xanthan gum

2 tablespoons chopped cilantro (optional)

½ teaspoon crushed red pepper flakes (optional)

salt and pepper, to taste

Cook's tip
The chopped, fresh cilantro adds an extra dimension to these wraps, but you can also use parsley.

PREP TIME: 15–20 minutes COOK TIME: 25 minutes MAKES: 8

Potato MUFFINS

These tasty muffins are best eaten straight from the oven and are a great addition to a cooked breakfast.

1 Preheat the oven to 350°F. Grease eight sections of a muffin pan.

2 Scoop the flesh out of the potatoes and mash until smooth. Make up the egg replacer in a small bowl according to the package directions, and beat it with a fork for a minute, until bubbly.

3 Put the margarine and sugar into the bowl of an electric food mixer and cream together. Alternatively, put the margarine and sugar into a large mixing bowl and cream together with a handheld electric mixer or a fork. Then add all the remaining ingredients and continue to mix until all the ingredients are just combined. Overmixing can make the potato sticky, so just make sure that the egg replacer and chives are well distributed.

4 Divide the batter between the prepared sections of the muffin pan and bake in the preheated oven for 25 minutes, or until crisp and golden.

- 2 medium baked potatoes
- vegan and gluten-free egg replacer, equivalent to 2 eggs
- ⅔ cup firmly packed vegan and gluten-free margarine, plus extra for greasing
- 2 tablespoons packed vegan light brown sugar
- 1⅓ cups gluten-free all-purpose flour
- 2¼ teaspoons gluten-free baking powder
- 3 tablespoons chopped fresh chives
- salt and pepper, to taste

Cook's tip

Leftover baked potatoes work well in this recipe, but you can use freshly boiled potatoes, too. You just need to make sure the potatoes are as dry as possible.

Beet MUFFINS

These unusual sweet-savory muffins are best served warm, spread with dairy-free butter or coconut oil.

1 Preheat the oven to 350°F. Line a 12-section muffin pan with paper cups.

2 Put the flour, baking powder, baking soda, xanthan gum, salt, cinnamon, and ginger into a large mixing bowl and stir together with a wooden spoon. Add the oil, agave nectar, and soy milk and mix well. Add the beets and stir until well combined.

3 Divide the batter equally among the muffin cups.

4 Bake in the preheated oven for 25 minutes, or until a toothpick inserted into the center of a muffin comes out clean. Let cool in the pan for 5 minutes before turning out onto a wire rack to cool.

1¾ cups gluten-free all-purpose flour

1½ teaspoons gluten-free baking powder

1½ teaspoons gluten-free baking soda

½ teaspoon xanthan gum

1 teaspoon salt

1 teaspoon ground cinnamon

1 teaspoon ground ginger

⅓ cup coconut oil

½ cup agave nectar

⅔ cup gluten-free soy milk

1 cup shredded raw beet

Cook's tip

Agave nectar adds sweetness without affecting the taste of the muffins. Coconut oil may be solid at cooler temperatures—if you need to melt it, let it cool before adding it to the mixture to stop the baking powder from acting too quickly.

Jalapeño Cornmeal MUFFINS

These muffins are best served warm, and are good with a hearty soup or vegan chili.

1 Preheat the oven to 350°F. Grease a 12-section muffin pan.

2 Mix the soy milk and cider vinegar together in a small bowl and set aside to curdle.

3 Put the cornmeal, baking powder, baking soda, and salt into a large mixing bowl and stir together with a wooden spoon.

4 Pour the curdled soy milk over the cornmeal mixture, add the applesauce, maple syrup, olive oil, and jalapeño, and quickly stir the mixture together. Divide the batter equally among the greased sections in the muffin pan and bake in the preheated oven for 20–25 minutes, or until a toothpick inserted into the center of a muffin comes out clean. Let cool in the pan for 5 minutes, then turn out and serve warm.

vegan and gluten-free margarine, for greasing

1 cup gluten-free soy milk

1 tablespoon vegan and gluten-free cider vinegar

2 cups fine cornmeal

1 tablespoon gluten-free baking powder

1 teaspoon gluten-free baking soda

1 teaspoon salt

¼ cup gluten-free, unwaxed applesauce

3 tablespoons maple syrup

¼ cup olive oil

1 unwaxed jalapeño pepper, seeded and chopped

Herb BISCUITS

These biscuits are best served hot, straight from the oven with dairy-free butter or freshly roasted garlic cloves.

1 Preheat the oven to 400°F. Grease a large baking sheet.

2 Put the flour into a large mixing bowl. Rub in the margarine, using your fingertips, until the texture is like soft bread crumbs. Stir in the baking powder, herbs, yeast flakes, and pepper. Add the soy milk and stir the mixture with a wooden spoon to make a soft, sticky dough.

3 Turn the dough out onto the greased baking sheet and use a spatula to shape it into a circle. Use a sharp knife to mark it into eight sections and sprinkle the poppy seeds over the top.

4 Bake in the preheated oven for 15–20 minutes, or until cooked through and a toothpick inserted into the loaf comes out clean. Let cool on the sheet for 5 minutes, then cut into sections and serve warm.

2 cups gluten-free all-purpose flour

¼ cup firmly packed vegan and gluten-free margarine, plus extra for greasing

4 teaspoons gluten-free baking powder

2 tablespoons finely chopped fresh herbs, such as thyme and sage

2 tablespoons nutritional yeast flakes

pepper, to taste

¾ cup gluten-free soy milk

1 tablespoon poppy seeds

Cook's tip

You can use a mixture of fresh herbs or choose one of your favorites instead—sage, rosemary, and chives all work well.

Roasted Pepper CROSTATAS

These adaptable individual tarts are great for lunch at your desk or a picnic.

1 Preheat the oven to 375°F.

2 Spread out the bell pepper slices in a baking dish and drizzle with the oil. Bake in the preheated oven for 15–20 minutes, or until softened but not browning. Set aside to cool and leave the oven on.

3 To make the dough, put the flour, baking powder, yeast flakes, and salt into a large mixing bowl and stir with a wooden spoon to combine. Rub in the margarine with your fingertips, then gradually stir in the milk and use your hands to bring the mixture together as a soft dough.

4 Transfer the dough to a lightly floured board and knead it gently to form a smooth ball. Cut the dough into four equal pieces and roll each piece out to line and slightly overhang four 4½-inch round, loose-bottom individual tart pans. Don't trim away the excess dough.

5 Divide the roasted bell peppers between the four pans and gently fold the dough up over the filling.

6 Bake in the preheated oven for 20–25 minutes, or until golden. Serve hot or cold.

a mix of 5 unwaxed red, yellow, or orange bell peppers, seeded and sliced

2 tablespoons sunflower oil

DOUGH

2 cups gluten-free all-purpose flour, plus extra for dusting

2 teaspoons baking powder

2 tablespoons nutritional yeast flakes

pinch of salt

¼ cup firmly packed vegan and gluten-free margarine

⅔ cup gluten-free soy milk

Cook's tip

You could add vegan and gluten-free cheese to this dish—if you use a meltable type, place over the peppers before folding up and baking. If it's not meltable, cut into small cubes and mix with the roasted peppers before you fill the crostatas.

Seeded BREADSTICKS

Nutritional yeast flakes give a cheesy flavor to these versatile crunchy breadsticks.

vegan and gluten-free egg replacer, equivalent to 2 eggs

2½ cups gluten-free white bread flour, plus extra for dusting

2 teaspoons xanthan gum

2 teaspoons vegan superfine or granulated sugar

3 tablespoons nutritional yeast flakes

2 tablespoons olive oil

1 tablespoon pepper

2¼ teaspoons active dry yeast

vegetable oil, for greasing

1 tablespoon white sesame seeds

1 tablespoon black sesame seeds

1 Make up the egg replacer in a small bowl according to the package directions, and beat it with a fork for a minute, until bubbly. Divide the egg mixture into two equal portions. Set one portion aside to glaze the breadsticks with later.

2 If you have a breadmaker, load it with the flour, xanthan gum, sugar, yeast flakes, olive oil, one portion of the egg replacer, and the pepper. Sprinkle the dry yeast on top and add 1 cup of warm water (not too hot, or it will kill the yeast). Set the machine to a "dough" setting and start.

3 If you don't have a breadmaker, sift the flour and xanthan gum into a large mixing bowl. Add the dry yeast, yeast flakes, sugar, and pepper, and mix together with a wooden spoon. Use the spoon to make a well in the center of the bowl. Mix the olive oil and one portion of the egg replacer together with 1 cup of warm water in a small bowl. Pour this wet mixture into the well in the dry ingredients and use a wooden spoon to stir all the ingredients together. Dust a large cutting board with flour, turn the dough out onto the board, and knead it for 5 minutes, until it forms a smooth ball. Put the dough into a large bowl, cover with greased plastic wrap, and let rest in a warm place to rise for about an hour, or until doubled in size.

4 Preheat the oven to 425°F. Grease a large baking sheet and line with parchment paper.

5 Dust a large cutting board with flour and turn out the dough onto the board. Pat it into a large log shape and cut into 20 equal pieces. Gently roll each piece into a long thin stick, about 12 inches long, and transfer the breadsticks to the prepared sheet. Brush each stick with the reserved egg replacer and then sprinkle them with the black and white sesame seeds.

6 Bake in the preheated oven for 15 minutes, or until just golden. Let cool a little before transferring to a wire rack until firm.

Cook's tip

Make sure there are no lumps in your egg replacer mixture—these can leave some unsightly white marks when glazing your breadsticks.

Rosemary & Garlic BREADSTICKS

These breadsticks are tasty enough to be served on their own, without any dips. Serve with Italian food or offer them as a snack with drinks.

1 Make up the egg replacer in a small bowl according to the package directions, and beat it with a fork for a minute, until bubbly. Divide the egg mixture into two equal portions. Set one portion aside to glaze the breadsticks with later.

2 If you have a breadmaker, load it with the flour, xanthan gum, sugar, olive oil, and one portion of the egg replacer. Sprinkle the dry yeast on top and add 1 cup of warm water (not too hot, or it will kill the yeast). Set the machine to a "dough" setting and start.

3 If you don't have a breadmaker, sift the flour and xanthan gum into a large mixing bowl. Add the dry yeast and sugar, and mix together with a wooden spoon. Use the spoon to make a well in the center of the bowl. Mix the olive oil and one portion of the egg replacer together with 1 cup of warm water in a small bowl. Pour this wet mixture into the well in the dry ingredients and use a wooden spoon to stir all the ingredients together. Dust a large cutting board with flour, turn out the dough onto the board, and knead it for 5 minutes, until it forms a smooth ball. Put the dough into a large bowl, cover with greased plastic wrap, and let rest in a warm place to rise for about an hour, or until doubled in size.

4 Preheat the oven to 425°F. Grease a large baking sheet and line with parchment paper.

5 Dust a large cutting board with flour. Sprinkle the rosemary and garlic powder over the flour. Turn out the dough onto the board and knead it until the rosemary and garlic powder are well incorporated into the dough. Pat it into a large log shape and cut into 20 equal pieces. Gently roll each piece into a long thin stick, about 12 inches long, and transfer the breadsticks to the prepared sheet. Brush each stick with the reserved egg replacer.

6 Bake in the preheated oven for 15 minutes, or until just golden. Let cool a little before transferring to a wire rack until crisp.

vegan and gluten-free egg replacer, equivalent to 2 eggs

2½ cups gluten-free white bread flour, plus extra for dusting

2 teaspoons xanthan gum

2 teaspoons vegan superfine or granulated sugar

2 tablespoons olive oil

2¼ teaspoons active dry yeast

vegetable oil, for greasing

2 tablespoons finely chopped fresh rosemary

1 tablespoon garlic powder

Cook's tip

If you want to try using other herbs, it's always best to use dried instead of fresh herbs so you can avoid adding any unwanted moisture to the dough.

Cracker BITES

These crispy little crackers make a guilt-free snack—use a selection of small cookie cutters to make a variety of pretty shapes.

1 Preheat the oven to 350°F and cover a large baking sheet with parchment paper.

2 Put the flour, yeast flakes, and thyme into a large mixing bowl and season with salt and pepper. Stir the mixture with a wooden spoon to combine.

3 Stir in the oil and gradually add ⅓–½ cup of cold water. Use your hands to bring the mixture together to form a dough that is soft but not sticky.

4 Turn out the dough onto a lightly floured board and roll it to about ⅛ inch thick. Use a small cookie cutter (1–2 inches in diameter) to cut out the crackers and place them on the prepared baking sheet. Reroll the dough scraps and make as many crackers as you can.

5 Bake in the preheated oven for 15–18 minutes, or until just golden on the bottom. Let the crackers cool on the baking sheet for a few minutes, then use a spatula to transfer them to a wire rack to cool.

1⅓ cups gluten-free all-purpose flour, plus extra for dusting

3 tablespoons nutritional yeast flakes

1 teaspoon dried thyme

3 tablespoons canola oil

salt and pepper, to taste

Index